the **single parent's handbook**

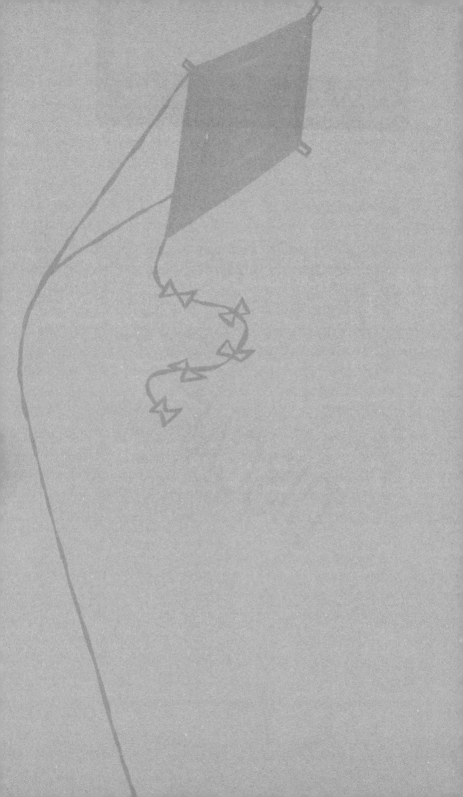

the single parent's handbook

Rachel Morris

PEARSON

Prentice Hall

LIFE

Pearson Education Limited
Edinburgh Gate
Harlow
Essex CM20 2JE
England

© Rachel Morris 2007

First published 2007

The right of Rachel Morris to be identified as author of this Work has been asserted by her in accordance with the Copyright, Designs and Patents Act, 1988.

Some names and location details have been changed to protect identities.

ISBN: 978-0-273-71283-1

Commissioning Editor: Emma Shackleton
Project Editor: Patricia Burgess
Text and Cover Design: Annette Peppis
Production Controller: Franco Forgione

Printed and bound by Henry Ling, UK

The Publisher's policy is to use paper manufactured from sustainable forests.

contents

To Mum

And Josh

Introduction

Television and newspapers like to refer to their specialised pre-senters and writers as 'experts'. I'd like to make it clear right away that, despite my media credentials, I don't consider my-self an expert on anything in life, least of all you, your parenting methods or your children. No amount of study or experience could qualify me or anyone else to tell you how to bring up your kids or run your home. Most single parents, including me, are doing their best under really difficult circumstances. We do not need to be told by someone we've never met, who has no idea about our individual circumstances, that we should be doing it differently. What I've tried to do in this book is share some of the insights that my personal and professional experi-ence have afforded me in the hope that they will be useful to other single parents facing the same kinds of issues. *The Single Parent's Handbook* is a pool of shared information, encour-agement, hassle-saving tips and lessons learnt from mistakes made by single parents who have gone before you, and its real value is in the wisdom that comes only with hindsight.

I grew up in a single-parent family as the eldest of five children, and was still a teenager when I became a mother myself. By the time I was 21, I had a single-parent family all of my own. But most of what I've learnt about families comes from the hundreds of hours spent as a psychotherapist listen-ing to clients talk intimately about their experiences of growing up and the issues raised by bringing up their own kids. While each individual's experience is obviously different, the same emotional issues often lie at the heart of the matter, and I've been able to pick out some of the most common threads and expand on them here.

Raising kids is stressful enough under the best of cir-cumstances. In today's society, where being a full-time parent is rarely respected as a career choice, and working parents are often vilified for putting their careers before their kids, it's hard to feel as though there's any way to win. As single parents, we have to face all the same issues as our couple counterparts – and then some. Being solely responsible for meeting all our children's needs, sometimes with very little support or acknowledgement, can feel burdensome, and that's not how most of us want to experience our children.

I believe a lot of the stress associated with being a single parent is born of having expectations of ourselves that are way too high. Each time we fail to meet our own criteria for being a 'good parent', we experience a sense of failure, high levels of anxiety, and a horrid gut-clawing guilt. The trick is to make our expectations reasonable by putting them in context with what we can actually achieve.

If we want things to be different, we have to be prepared to do things differently, but first we need to figure out which things we *can* change (so we can get on with changing them) and which things we're totally powerless to control (so we can stop wasting precious energy trying to alter the unalterable). It's the difference between running on a treadmill or running cross-country – they're both equally tiring, but one leaves you running on the spot, going over the same old ground again and again in a frustrating, stagnating cycle, and the other is an exhilarating journey taking you to new places with different terrains to negotiate. I've run both. The treadmill is exhausting and boring, but it can feel safe because when we don't believe in ourselves, we often choose the devil we know.

It takes courage to run without knowing where you're going. This book invites you to look at your situation through new eyes, to give you an opportunity to get some different ideas and a fresh approach to your circumstances. My hope is that, even though it takes more time to change things in the first instance, the changes you make will actually reduce stress so that you find there's more time to be the kind of parent you want to be and that your kids deserve to have.

I wouldn't advise you to read this book cover to cover. There's 16 years' worth of parenting issues to take in, so don't let it overwhelm you by trying to absorb it all at once. Also, there might be times when you come across an observation or a piece of advice that seems so obvious it'll make you want to slap your forehead and cry out, 'Why didn't I think of that?' Don't give yourself a hard time: remember, it's my job to make things simple, but at no point do I suggest that they are easy. The fact that you're trying is testimony to your desire to be a better parent, so be kind to yourself while you're reading what's contained in these pages. You might disagree with, or even feel outraged by, something I say. If so, feel free to ignore it. If your instincts tell you that a piece of advice is wrong for you, trust them; they're usually right. Your family is unique, and you know your own child better than anyone. I hope I've illustrated that we have more than one option when it comes to responding to our kids and the issues that being a single parent raise; that we're not trapped into behaving in the way we always have, or the way our own parents did.

The poet Philip Larkin famously said that parents f**k up their children. Well, he was right – we do – not because we're bad parents, but because children are as malleable as warm wax: we cannot handle them without leaving an imprint. I once asked an eminent child psychologist, mother of five and experienced therapist, that if she had just one piece of advice for parents, what it would be. She said, 'Accept that you'll make mistakes, forgive yourself for them in advance, and keep your fingers crossed you get away with them!'

It starts
with you

1
2
3

A few years ago I took a long-haul flight overseas. The safety video playing on the screen in front of me showed a smiling flight attendant demonstrating how to fit an oxygen mask to a child's face, while the voice-over effectively said that in the event of all the air being sucked out of the plane, adults were required to secure their own masks before helping children with theirs. It struck me as an unnatural request to make of a parent. It sounded all wrong, selfish even. What kind of parents make saving themselves a priority over their children? The answer is 'parents who want to be fit and able to protect their kids to the best of their ability'.

You first

If we really want to be the best parents we can be, we need to take the best possible care of ourselves. That might sometimes mean prioritising our needs over the needs of the children. For a lot of parents, mothers especially, this could come as a surprise, and might feel as though it contradicts everything we were taught about our role within the family. It's been only two generations since almost all mothers stayed at home while their husbands went out to work. Feminism, equal pay and equal rights have been issues only since the 1970s – less than 40 years ago. As single parents, we don't have the luxury of deciding which role we'll play in our kids' lives because once at home, we're all they've got, and we must play them all: homemaker, provider, nursemaid, disciplinarian and teacher to name just a few. Single or not, most of us feel inadequate as parents because while we recognise that we cannot be everything to our kids, we think we owe it to them to try, and often feel guilty when we fail.

There were many occasions when I was bringing up my son that time, money and energy were in extremely short supply, and I remember clearly just how guilty and selfish I felt whenever I took even the smallest slice of any of those resources for myself. On the other hand, I found that no matter how much I gave or 'gave up' for my son, it was never enough: he always needed more. As a young mum with the best of intentions, I felt incredibly frustrated and occasionally resentful towards him for that. Sometimes I would bark at him for daring to ask for one more story or five more minutes at the park. Then I'd feel consumed by guilt and regret for shouting at him, and end up giving him what he wanted anyway because I felt bad for being grumpy. The tears of shame and frustration I cried alone long after he was asleep made for a pretty tragic picture. I was young and proud and I didn't ask for help or seek support. I didn't wonder what *I* needed in order to make me a better mother; I simply asked myself what was wrong with me that I was finding it so hard. I felt ashamed and therefore kept my struggle to myself.

Thinking about that time fills me with sadness. It was so unnecessary and such a waste of precious time. Those childhood years go by so quickly. It's a huge regret of mine that I didn't learn how to enjoy being a parent because I was so busy trying to survive it. I had decided that I needed to be twice the parent in order to make up for the lack of a father, who by now had moved to the other end of the country and no longer had any regular input as a parent. I was already doing my best, and now I was expecting myself to be twice that. How can a person do twice their best? I had set myself up to fail by expecting more of myself than was actually possible to achieve – and I had only one child to consider. I can't even imagine what it must have been like for my mother. She was a single parent for most of my childhood. (Having a boyfriend or even remarrying didn't change this fact. We were her kids, and while we might have called our new stepfather 'Dad', we knew he was a parent in name only.) I'm the eldest, and by the time I was ten and she was 30 there were five of us, one of her and no such thing as the Child Support Agency or Family Credit. Prioritising needs was neither complicated nor emotional. For her it was painfully simple: work hard, feed and clothe the kids, pay the rent and heat the house – in that order. As far as she was concerned, needs other than food, warmth and shelter were frivolous luxuries. Being able to ponder what lies beyond survival means we are thriving.

That parents must make occasional sacrifices for their kids is a given. Two-parent families get to argue about whose turn it is to meet their children's needs, but when you're on your own, the job of deciding whose needs get met when is trickier. How do you look into the faces of your little darlings and decide to meet your needs over theirs? I've worked with parents, especially mums, who, with noble intentions, saw to their own needs so little that they found themselves not only resenting the role of parent, but resenting their kids too.

Just as sacrificing too much is self-defeating and potentially damaging to our relationship with our children, so is not sacrificing enough. We live in a very defensive society at the moment, where the underlying question I hear most often is 'What about me?' Not making enough room in our lives for our kids can leave them feeling as though they are an unwanted inconvenience, and while this might seem obvious, the ways in which we can accidentally squeeze our kids can be subtle and hard to see. If you're a person who finds it difficult to allow yourself the right to have and meet your needs, you're likely to experience an unreasonable amount of guilt about the times when you do give in to them. Guilt makes us feel defensive and angry, and we then direct those feelings at the kids because it feels as though they are making us feel that way and we resent them for it. We shout at them, which makes us feel bad, and so the cycle begins.

Case: Jenny and Sam

Jenny, a client of mine, had been a single and supremely sacrificing parent since her son Sam had been three years old. She didn't date, work or socialise for fear of not being the best mum she could be. When Sam was eight, Jenny fell in love with Pete, whom she'd met online. After a while she introduced him to Sam, and eventually Pete moved in with them. Jenny came to see me because she was worried about Sam. Her lovely, sweet little boy had turned into a 'little monster'. He was sulky and disobedient at home, quiet and withdrawn at school. He'd got into fights with his cousins, had stolen money from Jenny's purse, and regularly refused to get up in the morning or go to bed at night. She had expected a certain amount of fallout from Pete moving in, but she hadn't been prepared for Sam's more extreme behaviour.

She described how she'd taken a softly, softly approach in the beginning, but her patience had run out. She said she was worried, but what I saw was anger and resentment. When I challenged her, it all came tumbling out. 'Yes, I'm angry. Can't I have anything for myself? I gave up everything for Sam when his father left. I've totally devoted myself to his happiness, and apparently I'm not allowed any happiness of my own. He's so horrible to Pete, I feel ashamed of him.' Then she broke down in tears. 'Now I feel like a terrible person. He's just a little boy. It's me who should be ashamed. I should be putting him first, but I really love Pete. Why shouldn't I have what I want?' She felt Sam was forcing her to choose and she was trapped in a need/anger/

guilt cycle. Once I'd reassured her that she had every right to fall in love and have a relationship, and that she didn't have to choose at all, she was able to relax and begin to unravel the tangled threads of emotion.

Sam was 'acting out' his feelings because eight-year-olds don't have the emotional vocabulary or ability to express their feelings verbally. He couldn't tell Jenny how he felt – he could only show her. Like most children, he was probably afraid of the changes this relative stranger, who was muscling in on his mum's time and attention, would inevitably impress on his life. Sam had simply learnt a new way of ensuring that he remained the focus of his mum's attention – for better or worse! Simply put, Jenny was too busy feeling guilty to help her son adjust to the changes in their lives, which only reinforced his feelings of rejection, thus compounding his fears.

Does Jenny have a right to a love life? Yes, of course. Does Sam have a right to feel threatened and afraid? Absolutely. If we can accept that meeting our needs will impact on our children, we can settle into the task of supporting them through the changes.

It's important to remember that our kids' needs are endless, that they will always want 'one more' of whatever's on offer, whether it's time, love or money. Take that for granted and it's easier to accept that we can only give what there is to give.

I hope that it's become clear, if it isn't already, that we have more to give when we allow ourselves a life too, without guilt and without shame. Being a parent will not even begin to replace all that previously defined us. If spontaneity, ambition, stilettos, sports cars and sleeping late were your thing before the kids came along, chances are you're going to need some amount of those things afterwards too. It's all a question of degree.

Your needs

When I refer to 'needs' I mean the elements of life that make us feel supported and appreciated – the things that help us to grow and develop as people. We need comfort, reassurance and affection, stimulation, challenge and excitement. We need to feel autonomous and in control of our lives. We need to feel as though we have choices, the power to make our own decisions, and the right to change our minds. We need to rest. We need to feel like good people doing our best for our kids. We need nourishment – socially, intellectually and romantically. We need to feel we are living our lives and fulfilling our potential. This is no mean feat, I know, but I believe all these things are within reach if only we have the courage to reach in the first place.

In families with two parents, one takes the strain of meeting the children's needs, while the other takes the time to focus on themselves for a short while – thus each parent regularly engages in adult activities that both stimulate and nourish them as people as well as parents. Well, that's the idea. The reality of dual parenting can be very different; ask any couple! When listening to one part of a couple complaining that the other doesn't pull his or her weight, I often think that it's simpler for single parents. For us there's no question of waiting for someone else to pick up the slack, or stamping our feet until our significant other hears our pleas for equal parenting. There is no battle for us to enter about whose turn it is to pick the kids up from school, get up in the night, or do the shouting. We know it's down to us, and while that might sometimes be terrifying, annoying or lonely, knowing that there's no one else means we just get on with it.

The problems occur when we don't attend to ourselves too. Just because there's no one to argue with doesn't mean we should give up fighting for the right to a break, to some adult company, or to exploring our potential outside the home. But first we have to identify our opponent: who do we have to fight to get our needs met? The answer is – ourselves. We have to fight the temptation to give into the feeling that we aren't allowed to make our needs more important more often. We must ignore the clawing guilt that sometimes lies around the corner of everything we do that doesn't have our kids as the central focus. It's not uncommon for single parents to put their own needs aside for years in order to meet the endless demands of their children, only to wake up one day (after the kids have grown up and gone) with 'empty nest syndrome' – a depression characterised by a deep sense of loss and purpose-lessness. While we make children the centre of our universe, they do not make us the centre of theirs for very long, which is just one of the reasons why it's important that we don't allow ourselves to disappear completely into the role of parent.

Kids don't want martyrs; they want parents they can trust to take care of themselves so that they don't have to feel responsible for our well-being. When there are two parents, children usually assume that the adults will take care of each other, so the child feels at liberty to be a child, free of adult responsibilities and grown-up worries. Where there is only one parent, a child may feel it's his job to fill the shoes of the absent parent. It's understandable that occasionally single parents might actively welcome this from their kids, especially if they are unsupported and lonely, but we must resist the temptation to use our children as replacement companions, helpers or confidantes. In my experience, children who grow up in the supporting role tend to become adults who find it difficult to meet or even recognise their own needs. They also have difficulty forming equal relationships, and often find themselves in professions where 'caring' is the central theme: counselling, nursing, medicine, social work and the priesthood are full of grown-up, over-responsible children who only ever learnt how to care for other people. Others often report finding themselves in romantic relationships with alcoholics, gamblers, serial philanderers and other seemingly lost causes. The role that we choose to play in life is often moulded for us in childhood.

As I've mentioned, my mother was a single parent with five children. She was a vibrant, beautiful woman and would often lament her 'other' life, the one she would have lived had she not had children. She was an actress and once auditioned for the role of Deidre Barlow (then Langton) in *Coronation Street*. Family lore states that she got the job, but couldn't accept it because she fell pregnant with me. I'm sure this is an exaggeration, but at the time I heard this I was mortified to have been the reason that those bright lights never shone for my mum.

Being painfully aware of the sacrifices my mother made for us every day, I tried to make myself need less from her and tried hard to meet the needs of the little ones in order to reduce their demands on her. She came to rely on my help and eventually took it for granted. My role as helper got sown into the fabric of our family life so that I couldn't change it even if I wanted to. I remember asking when I was 15 if I could go to the school disco that Friday night. As that was one of the nights my mother worked as a waitress, and it was my job to look after my brother and sisters while she was out, she said I could go as long as I could find and pay a babysitter to replace me. I couldn't do either. I was trapped – between our need as a family for my mum to work, my role as childminder, and by my desperate desire to be a normal teenager.

THEY WILL NOT DO AS WE SAY; THEY WILL DO AS WE DO. If we want our children to grow into self-assured people with a clear idea of who they are, what they want, what they deserve and the will to work for it, we have to figure out how to be that for ourselves first. Share the process of your ongoing development so that they can see you're a work in progress, just like them. You will be showing them how to talk to you about their growing and changing circumstances, and it's much more powerful than telling them.

This all makes me sound like Cinderella in a fairy tale. But I was neither gracious nor patient about my situation. I was angry and sulky all the time and rowed frequently with my mum. I was certainly no martyr. I did it because I had no choice. I lived in fear for my family's survival, and felt, correctly, that I had a huge role to play in what felt like a fine dividing line between success and collapse. It has taken a fair amount of therapy to undo some of those ingrained beliefs, and it's for this reason that I am so passionately convinced that children need to feel that you, as their only parent, are happy, nourished and well supported. It's our job to do whatever it takes to achieve that so that we can then model it to our children.

The four corners of stability

Support, emotional nourishment, security and self-esteem are the four basic requirements for happiness. If we can learn how to get these needs met, not only will we have these things to pass on to our children, but life will become more enjoyable, more challenging and more enriching all round – and who doesn't want their children to grow up in that kind of positive and productive atmosphere?

The most direct routes to getting these needs met also happen to be the four areas that single parents feel, and often are, most excluded from.

Love life   Family life   Social life   Work life

If these were the four legs to a table that represented you, and each one was working – you had a good relationship, fantastic friends, a supportive family and a satisfying job – imagine how safe you would feel in your life. For some people it may be possible with time and effort to secure all four legs to stability, while some really lucky folk have all four without even seeming to try. However, for most single parents each leg presents its own unique set of problems, and plenty of us have had to make do with less than four legs to our table.

Take the first leg… Finding a partner isn't easy for anyone, but having children makes it feel more out of reach. It's all well and good saying that being in a relationship is one way of feeling supported, but in the case of parents who find themselves single as a result of bereavement or the breakdown of a relationship under violent or abusive circumstances, climbing back into the saddle and finding new love is unlikely to be on the menu for a long time as healing has to take place first.

As for the second leg… Employment issues are vast and hugely stressful for most single parents who want to work. According to the statistics, 90 per cent of single parents are women, and of those, 62 per cent are living on the poverty line, which isn't surprising when you take into consideration that childcare costs make most middle-income jobs not worth doing, and low-paid jobs often leave the parent bringing in less money than when they were claiming benefits (which was barely enough to survive on in the first place). Of course, some people choose to be full-time parents and regard their job to be child rearing.

Hardly anyone considers the third leg because our social life is seen as frivolous and expendable, but I believe it's essential if we're to hold on to our sense of identity. Maintaining our old friendships and exploring new ones helps us to remember who we are when we're not being Mum or Dad. In our children we see ourselves reflected as loving, caring, protective, organised and playful, but it's our friends who show us that we're witty, intelligent, charming, sexy and interesting too. For most of us, the issue of 'making friends' is scary and difficult. Where do you meet people? Will they find you interesting? Will you find them interesting? How will you initiate a conversation? Starting from scratch can feel like such a mountain to climb that lots of us don't bother, finding it easier to stay at home and hide behind our children's needs. But hiding denies us access to what could potentially be a tremendous corner of support.

As for the family leg… An awful lot of people have little or no family support at all, and without this leg in particular, access to other means of support becomes even more distant. Who else can you rely on to take care of your children at a moment's notice and not charge you for the privilege? While I was pregnant with my son, my mother and grandmother were tragically killed in a car accident together. A couple of months before that, my partner's family had emigrated to Australia. My brother and sisters were still young, so my stepfather had his hands full and was in dire need of support himself. One of the legs to my table was broken, and I would have to do without it for a very long time.

A three-legged table functions perfectly well as long as the legs are pretty firm. A table that has only two legs is far from stable, and the loss of one more means certain collapse. A person who lives with only two of these supports in place feels permanently insecure and is hypervigilant. It's for this reason that I now discuss these four areas in detail – what they might mean to you and how you might get some of those needs met in each of them, despite the challenges of being a single parent.

Love life

Romance, love and sex are modern preoccupations and difficult to escape or avoid. Whether you've only just come out of the relationship with your child's other parent or have been single for ages, the hole that being without romantic love leaves behind can feel gaping and terrifying when you've got children. Suddenly you're a package, not a person, and every date feels like you're interviewing candidates for the job of step-parent. That's assuming, of course, you've managed to find a babysitter you can afford to pay so that you can go out in order to meet someone to date in the first place. And it's also assuming that you've managed to come to terms with the end of your previous relationship, even though you have to see and speak to your ex all the time.

Dating – a whole new ball game

Revisiting the dating world as a parent for the first time can be a deeply unnerving experience no matter how much of a social butterfly you used to be. The first time I went out again with a group of female friends I remember feeling very anxious. My confidence and self-esteem were pretty low, and having been out of the loop for a while, I was worried that I'd feel like

IF IN DOUBT, DO NOWT!

It's good advice, this Yorkshire saying. Putting yourself under pressure will just make you feel stressed and anxious. You may feel lonely and miss the arms of a loving partner, but if you're not ready, you're not ready. Don't think about it for a month or two, but do keep reviewing it. The one thing that can always be said for feelings is that they are constantly changing, and what was true a week ago might not be true today.

a misfit. I hadn't bought any new clothes for ages, and in the company of friends who were single and childless (i.e. wealthy and carefree), I felt frumpy, grumpy and mumsy. I made the best of what I had and went out, despite not feeling comfortable in my clothes or my skin. I had an awful night. I was nervous. I talked too much, too fast and announced my single-parent status as if it were my surname to every bloke I was introduced to, which, as it turns out, isn't a great way to start a conversation.

I told myself that it had all gone wrong because I was a single parent. How can you relax when you've got to be home by midnight to relieve the babysitter? The experience put me off trying again for some time, but I can now see that I just wasn't ready to brave meeting someone new and risk putting my son and myself through the mill again. Having a child made me feel all the more vulnerable. My cards would have to be on the table from the start. I wanted to meet a man I could share a life with – just not yet.

The break-up

Painful break-ups knock everyone's confidence and self-esteem, but for a parent there are so many more ways to feel heartbroken, scared and bereft, and it's not just our feelings that need careful handling. Our kids need us to help them deal with their upset feelings too. Having the space to process a relationship ending is a luxury to a lone parent. Unlike the break-ups we experienced before having kids, where we got to lie on the sofa for days on end, crying into a vat of red wine, swearing we'll never love again, being a lone parent means putting your misery on hold every five minutes to deal with your four-year-old saying 'Please don't cry, Mummy', or your 14-year-old (who's too scared to mention his other parent's name in case you get upset again) thundering up and downstairs with his mates. There's no compassionate leave or sick days you can pull from being a single parent. This, along with having to see and make regular contact with the ex to sort out maintenance payments, access arrangements and so on, can make it feel impossible to do any moving on at all. But move on we must.

Once burnt, twice shy

Human beings are hardwired to avoid pain, both physical and emotional. During our childhood most of us will have burnt ourselves on a hot iron. Lots of us may even remember doing it twice, but very few will remember it happening three times because our brains form neurological pathways – connections between events and pain. If your best friend held out an iron and asked you to place your palm on the steel plate, your instinctive reaction would be to recoil from it. Even though you entirely trust your friend, your brain refers to an old file marked 'Iron = Burn' and sends a message that feels like an impulse or instinct – to withdraw. Of course, as adults we can choose to allow our judgement to override our instinct, but if we lose confidence in our own judgement, which is common after a break-up, we fall back on instinct to make our decisions for us. Emotional pain forms similar neurological pathways, which is part of the reason why, after a painful split, even thinking of meeting someone new can create a strong urge to run in the opposite direction and keep running. We need to remember that instincts are sometimes more biological than logical and can't always be trusted or believed.

Moving on

The past is a known quantity, and no matter how bad it's been, 'it's the devil you know' and is therefore more comfortable than a future we can't see because our biggest fear is of the unknown. This is why we hold on to the past. In order to move on, we need to have a sense of where we're going, what direction to take, and this is where you really get to play with the possibilities. Using your imagination, let yourself explore hopes and dreams for yourself. The following exercise will help you to decide what you want, then all you'll have to do is keep your eyes on the prize, putting one foot in front of the other until you get close enough to take it.

Take three deep, slow breaths, relax, close your eyes and imagine yourself in your life as it is today. Now fast-forward your life five years to where you hope to be by then. Explore your new life, the fruits of your hard work. Where will you be living? What car will you drive? What will you do for a job? Are you with someone? How do you feel about your life? How do you feel about yourself? Don't be mean – let yourself have whatever you want. It's only a fantasy for now, so don't hold back.

When you can really see this imaginary life, walk around it and see how it makes you feel. Make sure that every element is exactly how you would wish it. Then take an imaginary photo of your future life and place it in an imaginary shirt pocket over your heart and fast rewind back to where you are today.

Whenever you need reminding of where you're going, just put your hand over the imaginary photo and close your eyes. It's all still there, the future you designed for yourself. Don't worry that you don't know how you're going to get there. Have you ever been driving a car or riding a bike when something catches your eye and before you know it, you find yourself steering towards it without meaning to? We have a strong will to follow our eyes, which means we will walk towards whatever we concentrate on. If you keep your eyes on your goals, you will move towards them. Similarly, if you choose to focus on negative things, you move towards them too. So allow yourself a dream or two.

The blame game

Our emotional life at best looks like a free-flowing river or a bubbling brook. Over the years the water wears the banks into unique shapes that reflect our emotional patterns. Some of us are dramatic, thundering rivers that race around bends, jumping and spraying over stones and boulders. Others seem so still, deep and unmoving that they appear more like lakes than rivers. All that matters is that the emotions are allowed to flow unhindered because it's when we try to build a dam to block an emotion or an emotional fact that the problems begin.

Sometimes we don't realise we're blocking. I felt huge anger during the separation from my son's father. I blamed him for everything – my living situation, my financial position, my loneliness and my fear of the future. I blamed him for my behaviour too: surely if he'd been the man I'd needed him to be I wouldn't be on my own? If I weren't alone, I wouldn't feel so stressed, and if I weren't so stressed, I wouldn't have just shouted at our son so unfairly and made him cry. I was stuck in an angry whirlpool that just went round and round.

Getting unstuck isn't easy, but if you ask yourself what the payoff is to the feeling you're stuck in, the answer won't be far behind. For me, as long as I held on to my outrage, everything was my ex's fault and I couldn't be held responsible for anything that was going wrong. More importantly, I didn't have to look at how guilty I felt towards them both for the decision I'd made to move our son away from his dad.

We can't hope to feel as though we're in control of our life while we're blaming someone else for the state of it. It wasn't until I started to take responsibility for my predicament that I was able make plans and create the life I wanted. The more control I had, the less angry I felt. The less angry I was, the less stressed I became. The less stressed I was, the less alone I felt. We need to have faith that as long as we're not turning a blind eye on ourselves and pretending our problems don't exist, the feelings we have today will change – eventually.

You're the boss of you

List ten decisions *you* made that contributed to your situation today. Then go through each one of them, remembering why you made that decision and why it was the best decision you could have made given the information you had at the time. Our decisions only seem bad under the spotlight of regret, but regret is a refusal to recognise that life is a learning process. Your decisions brought you to where you are now, and you know more now than you ever have. Knowledge is power. Thus all your decisions make you personally more powerful.

Ask for help

If you're happily single and have no intention of sharing your life with a lover, good for you. Everyone has the right to design their life according to their own needs, and I'm certainly not suggesting that finding love is the only route to fulfilment. If you're single because, even though you want to find love, you're just not ready, don't worry. Take the pressure off by telling yourself that you won't even think about it for three months, then revisit your feelings on the subject by talking to friends or, better still, a counsellor or psychotherapist. A professional can help you to understand more about your feelings and what you can do to change them if you want to. Your friends will help you to keep perspective. There's nothing wrong with asking for a little help. If you broke a leg, you'd rely on a crutch to get around until you felt strong enough to go it alone. Having your confidence damaged is far worse than breaking a leg, yet we expect ourselves to hobble along making the best of it, hoping it will heal itself.

The importance of touch

Whether alone through choice or not, single people often suffer a certain amount of tactile deprivation. Human beings need regular physical contact in both sexual and non-sexual contexts to maintain a sense of well-being. Intimate contact with other living creatures has a calming effect on us. Touch stimulates a chemical release into the pleasure centres of the brain that makes us feel reassured and safe. A recent experiment in the USA showed that the fear response in the brains of women under threat was vastly reduced when measured while the women were holding their partners' hand. Similarly, we know that stroking an animal can reduce blood pressure and raise a sense of well-being. As a result of these findings, it's not unusual to see 'pat' dogs in hospitals, on paediatric and geriatric wards. (Children need huge amounts of touch, and old people, who are often alone in later life, appreciate it too.)

Of course, relationships won't keep our blood pressure down (in my experience, they do just the opposite), but if we're without a romantic partner and we don't get those tactile needs met, we can wind up feeling isolated and lonely even if we're leading busy, active lives. Some folks are naturally touchy-feely types and will get lots of non-sexual contact from their friends and family, but others who perhaps come from backgrounds that don't display affection might find that the only real contact they have is with their children. While there's nothing wrong in that, the touching we share with our kids is generally for their benefit, not ours. When we start trying to get our needs met by our kids, we're in danger of putting pressure on them to take care of us. Children want above all else to please us, but not at the expense of pleasing themselves. They know which way around the parenting relationship should be, and when we try to reverse it, they soon let us know.

One bedtime my son, aged six, told me kindly yet firmly that he didn't want any more cuddles or stories. He thanked me politely and said if it was OK with me, he'd really like to go to sleep now. This made me realise that spending hours over his bedtime was more about me getting my cuddle quota and not wanting to face the long evening hours alone than it was about being a good mum. His rejection of my time and affection hurt my feelings, but woke me up to the fact that I needed more adult interaction, more intimately. Easy to say, much more difficult to implement, but after some amount of asking around (oh, how I mourn the lack of the Internet back then) I found a local college that ran training courses for massage, hairdressing and beauty therapies, and promptly offered myself up as a guinea pig for the trainees. It wasn't until I had my first aromatherapy massage that I realised how starved of touch I had been. I cried for a full hour afterwards. Being touched had made me realise just how lonely I really was, and how starved I felt of human closeness. Massage is a fantastic way of getting those needs met because it reduces stress on several levels, but salsa dancing remains my favourite means of achieving non-sexual human closeness. You get close physical contact with a member of the opposite sex, but in a non-threatening and fun way. Joining a gym or a class in yoga or Pilates are also great ways to meet people and relieve isolation, as you're a member of a group – but more about that later.

Nothing to offer

♦♦ *I went on a date recently and I had nothing to say. He had a really interesting job and all I had to offer was the latest on potty training techniques.* ♦♦

Lots of single parents have had similar experiences. I once attended a rare dinner party when my son was small. I was having a lovely chat with the perfectly nice man sitting on my right. All was well until I semi-consciously noticed that he was struggling to cut through a particularly tough piece of beef. Without missing a beat, I leaned over and began to cut it for him using my own knife and fork. It was clear – I needed to get out more. When I told a friend this story, she accused me of stealing it from her. Since then, I've heard it over and over in various guises. When kids are very young, they can be all consuming, and if we don't get regular adult breaks, their eating and toilet habits may well be all we have to share, which is just one of the reasons it's important to enjoy a sliver of life away from them.

Sex

Getting our sexual needs met outside a relationship can mean only one of two things: one-night stands or masturbation. I don't recommend one-night stands because they're like kebabs: they only seem like a good idea after a few drinks, are ultimately unsatisfying, and tend to leave you feeling slightly greasy and shameful. Woody Allen purportedly said, 'Sex without romance is an empty experience, but as empty experiences go, it's one of the best.' And I'm sure that on the odd occasion this might be true for all of us, but on the whole, it merely serves to make the lack feel greater.

I realise that sex is a delicate subject for lots of us, but I'm making a simple point: just because you don't have a partner right now doesn't mean that you're not a sensual being. Stay in the habit of thinking of yourself as such and don't fall into asexual habits because this will just make you feel even more removed from your adult self. If you're not sure whether this has already happened, take a look at your underwear drawer. Is it full of big, grey, rainy day knickers or is it vibrant and alive with sensuality and promise? Yup – thought as much! Don't make the mistake of thinking that if no one's going to see, then it doesn't matter what you wear. *You* will know. *You* will see yourself wearing them and it will affect the way you see yourself, which in turn affects the way others see you. That also goes for baggy leggings, jeans that are too short in the leg, shapeless sweatshirts, odd socks with trainers, and dressing gowns of all types. Dress as you want to feel instead of how you actually feel and you'll be surprised by the difference it makes to your confidence. This goes for men too; just because those boxer shorts still have a few threads holding them together doesn't mean they're not ready for the bin.

It's all in the attitude

◆◆ I have stretch marks and saggy breasts. Who will fancy me now? ◆◆

A woman's sexuality is all wrapped up in how fanciable she believes herself to be. When we feel gorgeous, we hold ourselves differently. We give off an air of confidence and sensuality that is noticeable and attractive to all. Men (under pressure) will admit to being attracted in the first instance to a woman's physical features, but it's her attitude, confidence and style that take their interest to a second stage. Most mortal men don't have x-ray vision, so your stretch marks can remain your secret for the time being, and a good bra can create all manner of wonderful illusions, as can magic tummy-

sucking pants and bum-shaping tights. Don't let the fear of being seen naked stop you from being the gorgeous sexy woman you know you are.

Get out there!

So you've put the past behind you and decided to bite the bullet, but where do you start and with whom? Singles the world over share the same dilemma if the plethora of Internet dating sites, newspaper lonely hearts columns and professional introduction agencies are anything to go by. This should be a comfort, but one of the most common feelings that accompanies loneliness is shame. As if it isn't bad enough feeling unloved and isolated, it seems we're deeply embarrassed by it and would rather stay miserable than come out and admit it. An admission of loneliness feels like an announcement of unlovableness. I believe this is an old hang-up from school. Kids who had few or no friends were pitied and regarded with suspicion by their peers. They were teased and sometimes bullied. Most of us will remember 'that kid' with a shudder.

The need for human contact is also a biological imperative – a throwback to cave times, when without other bodies to help us hunt, keep warm and defend our caves from sabre-toothed tigers, we were in deep trouble. These days, even though we have supermarkets, central heating and mortice locks, the innate fear of loneliness persists. Either way, this is one more of those less than helpful neurological pathways that we don't need any more. Loneliness is a temporary, recoverable state that doesn't mean imminent death or permanent social isolation. It's simply the recognition of a lack of intimacy; the symptom that spurs us on to find companionship because we generally fare better that way.

Safety first

OK, now you've got a handle on the loneliness thing, you can drop any negative feelings associated with needing to go on some dates, and just generally hang out with people whom you don't have to remind to eat with their mouths closed (I hope). Meeting someone through a lonely hearts column or an Internet dating site, or even on a night out, are all dates with a relative stranger. Not to spoil your fun or anything, but following a few guidelines will make you and your date feel safe.

♦ Never give personal details, such as your address, place of work or where your kids go to school, to someone you've just met, whether on the phone, the Internet or in person.

♦ Meet for the first time in a well-lit public place.

♦ Arrange the first meeting for an hour only. This means you don't have to waste an entire evening on someone you don't like or fancy. Don't worry about this causing offence; it goes both ways, after all.

♦ Practise saying 'Thanks but no thanks'. Lots of people find love through dating agencies, but most will tell you they had to meet a fair few before they met that special person. Be firm and fair.

♦ Be as honest as you feel like being. If you don't want to answer a question, don't. This is a stranger and should be treated as such.

♦ Listen to your gut instinct. If you get a funny feeling about someone, it's probably for a good reason. Listen to it and move on to the next person.

♦ Beware the single mum hunter. Like all predators of the animal world, they look for weakness in their victims – in this case, women who don't get out that often, who've lost some of their social confidence and are grateful and relieved for any male attention. Lap up the attention by all means – just remember that when your self-esteem isn't what it should be, flattery can lead you down a disappointing alley. If you don't trust your judgement, meet for coffee or lunch during the day. The absence of alcohol will help you get a better perspective.

Chat up!

♦♦ *I'm scared that if I tell a guy who's chatting me up that I've got kids, he'll run for the hills.* ♦♦

He might. Let's face it – not everyone's idea of a perfect date is someone who has to be back by midnight for the babysitter, but remember, you're just chatting and there's much more to you than being a mum. Try not mentioning it first. This will force you to talk about other aspects of your life, and if he's interesting enough to talk to for longer, tell him then. If he makes his excuses and leaves, let him go willingly. People are perfectly entitled not to want relationships with single parents. It's not personal, and the sooner you find out the better.

Be proud. People will take your lead as to how to feel about having kids. If you pass on the information as though you expect to be rejected for it, you're likely to come across as either apologetic or defensive, neither of which is a particularly attractive quality, and both give the impression that there's something to worry about. Being positive about your children will make other people feel at ease about them. Carry a photo to show proudly, and feel good about the job you're doing. If being a single parent doesn't appear to be troubling you, it has no reason to trouble anyone else.

DATING DOS AND DON'TS

♦ **Don't** apologise for being a single parent. Everyone agrees that parenting is the hardest job in the world, and you're doing it alone. Hold your head high. Your kids are an asset, not a burden.

♦ **Do** leave the kids at home. Use the time to rediscover the person you are when you're not being a parent.

♦ **Don't** worry you'll have nothing to say; just listen to begin with. There's nothing people find more flattering than someone who appears interested. Pick up on points of identification and similarity. Soon you're chatting!

♦ **Do** avoid interviewing your date on behalf of your children. Finding out how the other person feels about Teletubbies or the latest PS2 game is not required information on a first date.

♦ **Do** keep your boundaries firm from the beginning so that your date knows that your kids come first. If you have to be home by 11, don't make up excuses to hide the reality of dating a single parent. If things are going to progress, you will need that person's support.

♦ **Don't** bring dates home to meet your kids or stay the night until you feel confident that the relationship is going somewhere. I know this makes the beginning of a new relationship a bit tricky, but it's better than trailing a series of 'uncles' or 'aunties' through your kids' home.

♦ **Do** take the pressure off. A first date isn't a date at all. It's a meeting where two people see whether or not they like each other enough to arrange a proper date. A real date indicates romantic intention, which piles on the pressure. Besides, as desperate as you might feel for a bit of romance, that's not what's on the table at the first meeting, so relax and have fun.

Family life

Family is a complicated emotional labyrinth riddled with history both good and bad. It has nooks and crannies packed with unspoken truths, hidden hurts, quiet shame and dark skeletons. On the other hand, family can be a warm, enveloping quilt that keeps us safe from the world's ills. What does it mean to you, and what binds you to it? A sublime sense of belonging, or perhaps a suffocating sense of duty? One family has dozens of members; another has just two. One has four parents, while another has none. Some are easy to navigate, and others resemble a complex warren of unspoken rules. Religion, culture, class and economic status all contribute to the ever-changing face of the family, and if we want it to flourish, we have to be prepared to accommodate the changes. As unique as our experiences of family may be, there is one likely universal truth: that our lives are profoundly affected by its presence and its absence.

A precious commodity

For single parents who have it and feel they can lean on it free of emotional charge, family is the strongest corner on the table of stability. They are the lucky few because the rest of us, who certainly make up the majority, are nervously tiptoeing our way through minefields of complicated family dynamics, or desperately trying to create new families out of friends and neighbours. Even the privileged few rarely feel good about having to rely on parents or brothers and sisters who have their own lives to lead, but we don't always have a choice, which is why we need to learn to make the best of it. For some that will mean making just a bit more effort by picking up the phone more often, arranging visits and days out together, or perhaps letting go of a few meaningless old resentments. For others it could mean seeking expert help in the form of therapy or a support group.

Potentially, family is a priceless source of love and support. Most of us have 'issues' of some sort with our family, and while it takes enormous courage to confront painful feelings wrapped up in past events, it's worth doing everything you can to deal with them so that you can move on. A family in good working order is worth its weight in plutonium, and you owe it to yourself at least to try a new trick or two to improve yours.

Note: there are some family wounds that can't be 'fixed'. For those who were abused, neglected or abandoned, family is unlikely to be considered a place of support, and there are some situations where the best course of action is to walk away altogether. In this case, or any other where birth or adopted family is not an option, creating a brand new family of your own, made up of friends and support groups, can be a rich and fulfilling experience, and I highly recommend it.

Whether your family is a blood-related unit or a chosen group of trusted individuals, what you're dealing with is a network of delicate human relationships vulnerable to misunderstandings, breakdowns in communication, bickering, rivalry, jealousy, resentment and all manner of other normal, healthy feelings. That's why families need tender nurturing so that they can grow into big, strong support mechanisms capable of bearing the weightiest of burdens.

While my brother and sisters were too young to be of any support when my son was a baby, they are now rock-solid pillars of love and strength for him and me, but it didn't come easily. Our mother had been the heart of our family, and when she died we fell away like the petals of a flower. As we grew up, we grew apart in our own private worlds of grief. The love was always there, but the wisdom and the courage to face it all together and become a family again took ten years to accrue, and another ten to achieve.

It makes me shudder to remember how we've fought, the things we've said and done to one another, and the abandon with which we lashed out in retaliation. There have been long silent absences from each of us as we tried in our own way to grow up the best we could under the circumstances.

After my son, my siblings are the most important people in the world to me. They are also the only people (after my son) who can send me into a flying rage, make me argue like a four-year-old, frustrate me to the point of implosion, and ignite a murderous streak with the twitch of an eyebrow. Now that all five of us are aged between 30 and 40, it would be nice to think that we've matured to the point where we can be civilised with one another and put childish things behind us, but we haven't. I can imagine us bickering and delivering dead legs when we're all between 80 and 90, and I'll feel blessed for a lifetime of having them to lean on and to take things out on.

> ♦♦ *Nothing changes if nothing changes, but do one thing differently and nothing can be the same again. It's the law of dynamics.* ♦♦

Today we are firm friends, and our rows are limited mostly to short bursts of quick-fire rounds. Apologies no longer feel like vomiting razor blades, and these days we'd rather kiss and make up than stick pins in our eyes, which is a refreshing turnaround.

Assumptions

Making assumptions is one of the main causes of communication failure, and the total breakdown of a relationship can often be traced back to a solitary unchecked assumption.

I challenged one single mum, let's call her Jane, during a therapy session about her unwillingness to talk to her parents about how badly she felt for relying on them so much. 'I'm scared to start a conversation that might end in them pulling their support and admitting that it's too much for them. They're both retired, and looking after my kids three times a week probably wasn't what they planned for themselves, but I just can't do it without them right now.'

> **Assumption 1:** 'It's too much for them.'
> **Assumption 2:** 'They will pull their support.'
> **Assumption 3:** 'It wasn't what they'd planned.'

Jane had held these assumptions for so long that over time they'd solidified into facts in her mind. She was convinced she was ruining their hard-earned retirement, which made her feel guilty and ashamed. Unsurprisingly, being in her parents' company had become awkward, so she no longer stayed for tea when she collected the kids. Instead, she was in and out as quickly as possible. Once Jane found the courage to have the conversation, she was like a different woman, all light and freshly unburdened. She told me how shocked they were at her assumptions, and while it explained why she'd been withdrawing from them (they'd 'assumed' she was upset with them), she couldn't have got it more wrong. They loved having the children, and while it was hard work, it kept them feeling useful and youthful. They felt privileged to be able to bond with their grandchildren, and had no intention of not being there for them, or her, for as long as they were able.

Jane bounced the palm of her hand off her forehead and laughed. 'I can't believe I was so unhappy all those months for nothing!'

IS IT FEELING OR FACT?

Feelings can quickly turn into facts if we don't check them out. Assumptions lie just under the surface, subtly changing the nature of our relationships without our conscious awareness. So assume no more. Check, check and double-check. At best, you'll find out there isn't a problem at all. At worst, you'll blow everything out into the open and be forced to resolve the issue one way or another. Either way, you'll be relieved. Denial might seem convenient at the time, but ultimately it does more harm than good.

Just talk

'Talk' is the easiest advice in the world to give, and probably the most difficult to follow. Even if we know what we want to say, we might not know how to say it. We're afraid of getting into a row and saying things we don't mean, or things we *do* mean that might hurt someone we love. How do you keep calm when you feel angry? How do you not strike back when that loved one lashes out at you? One-up-manship, the blame game, you said I said, misunderstandings, assumptions, judgements and insults are all reasons we avoid getting too 'real' with our families. We'd rather forgive and forget, and if that's what we really did, I'd be all for it. The problem is that we neither forget nor forgive unless an honest and revealing conversation has taken place and a mutual agreement to let it go has been reached.

The conversation opposite will serve as a template to get you started.

Four-part 'I' message

Part 1: 'I have a problem. Can we talk?'

Note: '*I* have a problem', not 'I'm having a problem with *you*'. Owning the problem puts the other person at ease; it's not about them, it's about you. They are more likely to listen if you're asking for help than if you're gearing up for a row.

Part 2: 'When you…'

Describe the problem behaviour precisely without using provocative language. For example, 'When you don't do as I ask regarding the boys' routine…' as opposed to 'When you rudely disregard my instructions as if I didn't exist time and time again…'

Part 3: 'It makes me feel…'

Use emotional words to describe exactly how it makes you feel. For example, 'It makes me feel as though you don't believe in me or respect me as a mother. It leaves me frustrated and hurt. It makes me think that maybe you don't believe in me, and I need you to because I'm new at this. Just because I want to do some things my way doesn't mean I don't need you.' Make sure you stay talking about you and your feelings because the minute you stray into talking about the other person, you're inviting them to interrupt to set you straight.

Part 4: 'Will you help me…'

Asking for help defuses a potentially tricky situation. For example, 'Will you help me to

understand why it's happening and if there's
something I can do to help resolve the problem?'

If successful, you have managed to communicate that *you*
have a problem with an aspect of the *other person's* behaviour.
You've explained how it makes you *feel* and asked for
that person's help in understanding and resolving it.

Congratulations – you've just had an honest, argument-free discussion about a touchy topic with someone you love
– and they're still speaking to you.

OTHER TIPS ON TALKING

♦ Make a pact at the beginning of the conversation not
to argue. If your discussion starts to get heated, remember
you have options. You are not bound to end up fighting just
because you always have. Go for a walk to calm down. Offer
to make a cup of tea. Apologise for something you just said,
or for the way you said it. Breathe deeply and try again.

♦ Start every sentence with 'I'. Imagine your index finger is
permanently pointing and ask yourself regularly, to whom
is it pointing? If the answer is at the other person, you're
probably attacking, criticising and/or judging, and that's
fighting talk. Keep your finger pointed at you.

♦ Avoid old scripts. If your rows always end up in the same
place, it's because there is an unresolved issue between you.
Cut to the chase and talk about what's at the heart of the
matter so that you can move on and have new and different
arguments.

♦ Stay open to the fact that you could be wrong. See your
discussion as a joint investigation rather than a courtroom
battle.

♦ Say it out loud. If you feel hurt, don't hint at it by snapping or sulking; say, 'I feel really hurt/angry/resentful at that'.

Whose kids are they anyway?

" *I have four boys under ten, and my dad helps me out a lot since I split up with my husband last year. He's amazing with the kids, and they adore him, but he tends to undermine my authority in front of them all the time. How do I ask him to stop it without upsetting him?* "

By being direct and compassionate. He's a big, grown-up man and you have to trust that he can handle hearing the truth about how his behaviour is affecting you. Use the four-part 'I' message outlined on page 43 to challenge him on it. Dads traditionally feel jealous of their daughter's husbands because they take over as the man in your life. Now your partner's gone, he could be feeling very protective of you again, and what you call undermining, he might think of as sharing the burden. Point out that undermining your authority is informing the boys that they don't have to take you seriously, which is going to create huge problems for you in the future. As a woman raising boys, you might find that you regularly come up against sexist attitudes. Your dad might not think you can cope with four boys alone, and it's your job to stand up to him and show that not only can you deal with your boys, but you can deal with him too!

Conflict of interests

Your family is fantastic, your ex's family is fantastic. Everyone wants to help, and you're grateful for their support but – and here's the rub – they keep telling you how you could be doing it better/differently/more effectively. You really want to tell them to leave you alone; that if you wanted their advice, you'd ask for it, thanks very much. But you can't because you need them, you're beholden to them and you know they mean well, so you don't want to upset them. What do you do?

This was exactly the problem troubling one of my clients. Rita was married and divorced by the time her son Warren was three, and she's had to rely heavily on both her own and her ex-husband's parents to take care of him so that she could work and socialise. Having two sets of grandparents and his father all wanting to spend time with him has meant she's had pretty much every Saturday night/Sunday morning to herself, plus one, sometimes two evenings in the week. It's hard not to feel jealous when I think of my own support-starved experience.

'I know how lucky I am, and I've no idea how I'd have managed without them,' says Rita. 'I've always felt grateful for what they do for me, but it comes at a cost.' She went on to explain that she had her own ideas about how she wanted to raise Warren. She wanted to be able to make her own mistakes and learn her own lessons, but with so many experienced parents around her, she's had to battle to get her way, and often lost.

'When Warren was a toddler the in-laws regularly fed him chocolate and red meat behind my back, despite my sugar-free, vegetarian diet directive. I was furious when I found out, but how could I have a go at them when they were doing so much for me? They believed they were acting in Warren's best interests, and as crazy as that made me, I had to bite my tongue. It might sound mercenary, but I needed them. I still do!'

The compromises we sometimes have to make to get the help we need is part of the cost of being a single parent. 'Mercenary' is the last word I'd use to describe it. Feeling as though you have to give up the right to rear your child the way you want is a huge sacrifice. While Warren merely swallowed a few prohibited treats, Rita felt that she was being force-fed her pride. However, as a desperate woman, she felt beggars couldn't be choosers.

Warren is now 14, but conflicts still crop up. Recently Rita went on a four-day work trip abroad and had to leave him with her mum. On her second night away her mum called to inform her that Warren had a bad cold and would be having the following day off school. 'Mum!' Rita exclaimed. 'You should've spoken to me first. He's just pulling a fast one because he's got a test tomorrow.'

Her mum remained unmoved. 'Well, that may be, but he really isn't well. You're not here, I am, and I'm not sending him to school, test or no test.' Rita, frustrated and indignant, began to shout at her mum, who asked her to lower her voice. In response, she yelled into the receiver, 'Stop talking to me like a child. Warren's my son and I'm the boss of him, not you.' She told me she heard her mother's eyebrows rise in satisfaction from across Europe!

Hands up anyone who doesn't recognise this dilemma. Accepting active support from family can be like giving them carte blanche to proffer opinions on your kids' development and your parenting techniques, and to disregard instructions that conflict with their ideas. This is especially problematic with your own family. Telling your mum that you've decided to bring up your children differently from the way she brought you up might raise a paranoid question or two that you should be prepared to answer kindly but honestly.

I'll do it my way

** *My mum refuses to take me seriously as a parent. I know I'm a young mum, but I'm older than she was when she had me. I've been trying to follow the Gina Ford method with my twin boys, but she refuses to follow their routines on the days she has them. I really need her help, but I'm so angry with her.* **

Your mother is used to being The Mum in the family, and she might be finding it difficult to share the role. You need to tell her how it makes you feel, but first you have to spend a bit of time working out exactly what that is. 'Angry' is a kind of umbrella term that we sometimes use to mask our more vulnerable feelings, such as hurt and upset. What new mum doesn't need to feel 100 per cent supported by her mum? She clearly has a problem with your routine, and until you find out what that is, you haven't got a hope of resolving anything. Don't assume it's because she doesn't take you seriously. She might be hurt that you've turned to a book rather than to her for parenting advice. She might need some reassurance that you take her seriously. Explain what it is you like about the method, and buy her the book so she can study it in her own time too.

Say 'thank you'

Now that my son is nearly 20, friends who have younger children sometimes mistakenly believe that my parenting role is over. It's wishful thinking on their part. If we really understood that parenting is a lifetime's responsibility, we might never submit to it. I remember one mum during the filming of a *Little Angels* episode looking up at me and shouting over her toddler's ear-splitting screams, 'It gets better, right?' It was a plea for mercy. I asked her if she wanted the truth. She shook her head and said firmly, 'Not if the answer's no.'

The truth is that it gets different. The sleeplessness you suffered when they were babies is superseded by tantrums at two, which will be replaced by monsters under the bed at four, alienation at eight, angst at 14, sex at 17, alcohol at 19, and so on and so on. Before you dive under your duvet in despair, I tell you this only to make a point: becoming a parent yourself doesn't put you on an equal footing with your parents. No matter how big and clever you get, they will always see you not as a child, but as *their* child. Parents often continue to feel responsible for their kids long into adulthood and beyond. They still worry as much, but about different things. My son could be chief executive of a multi-million-pound corporation, with responsibility for a thousand jobs, and I'd still have to stop myself from making suggestions about how he could make his life run more smoothly.

When you feel angry with your parents for not getting it right, presently or in the past, look at your own child and feel that consuming combination of love, responsibility, guilt and fear. Now multiply that by how many more years your parents have loved you and you'll have some idea of how they feel. Be gentle with them. In 20 years' time, when your children are adults and the results of your parenting mistakes and successes are out there for all to judge, you might feel a little vulnerable too.

Thank your folks for all that they got right and for doing their best. Forgive them privately for the fact that their best wasn't always great and might have fallen short of the mark at times when you really needed them to get it right. If you can do this for them, you might one day be able to do it for yourself because you too will surely make mistakes that you hope your kids will forgive you for.

The ex's parents

In-laws, by which I mean your ex's parents, whether you were married or not, get a really raw deal, and while I'm sure there are times they deserve it, there are certainly times when they don't. They're blood relatives of our children and want to share their lives, but as they're not strictly related to us, and since we're no longer linked to them via their son or daughter, the position they hold in our family isn't assured. The in-laws are not to blame for the relationship breaking down, but they might have to bear the brunt of it. The rules of engagement all change, along with the circumstances, but will they have a role in their grandchildren's lives now that their own blood child is no longer a joint carer? Theirs is a very insecure position to be in, which goes some of the way to explaining why Granny and Grandad sometimes act a little strangely.

Back off, Grandma!

◆◆ *Dealing with my ex's parents is incredibly frustrating, mostly because I don't know them well enough to feel comfortable about confronting them on difficult issues. They're good people, but since I split up with their son six months ago, they've made a habit of dropping by without warning, bringing toys, clothes, books and even food for my three-year-old. I'm very strict with Ruby's diet because she has allergies, and I hate the clothes and toys they buy – they're so old-fashioned. I know they're just trying to be nice, but it's driving me crazy. Last week alone saw three unannounced visits, and they came bearing one of the ugliest dolls I've ever seen, one packet of dolly mixtures (they thought because they were little sweets that they probably weren't as bad for her!) and a lemon hand-knitted cardigan from a charity shop. I know I sound like an ungrateful bitch, but I just don't know how to deal with it. They're retired and have said that they're available for babysitting any time I want. I'd love to have Ruby collected from her nursery as work makes me late picking her up, but the idea of having to see them every day is more stressful than asking friends and other mothers to do it for me.* ◆◆

As this behaviour only came about after the split, there's a pretty good chance that it's just their reaction to it. It's obvious from the outside that they're trying their best to ingratiate themselves with you and getting it all wrong. What they need is direction, a conversation and a bit of reassurance that while you might not be 'with' their son any longer, you have absolutely no intention of coming between them and their grandchild. Once you've pushed that message home, they'll relax a little and you'll feel more confident about laying down a few ground rules and taking advantage of their kind offer.

I'm a little biased in favour of in-laws because I'd hate to end up on the sidelines as so many of them do. While I hope my son and the (imaginary) mother of his (imaginary) child(ren) live happily ever after in a nice little nucleus of family security, current UK statistics report that there's a one in four chance he'll become either a single dad or a weekend one, and only a 10 per cent chance that the child(ren) will end up with him. This will put me squarely in the position I'm describing – the ex-mother-in-law. As such, I insist we give them a fair go.

TIPS FOR HANDLING EX-GRANDPARENTS

♦ While you're busy biting your tongue in fear of offending them, they will be picking up all sorts of negative vibes from you. Your underlying irritation or frustration will come out in small ways that are almost guaranteed to confuse or upset them. Have it out. They're going to be around for quite a while.

♦ Sit down together and design the kind of routine that will suit all of you. It's an opportunity for you to talk about the role you would like them to take in your child's life, thus implying the areas you'd like them to keep out of.

♦ Choose your battles. Saying 'no' to everything is really unproductive. Compromise a little. If they love to see your little girl dressed in those (hideous) pink bloomers they bought for her birthday, would it really hurt you to let her wear them when she visits? Save the hard line for the stuff that really counts.

♦ Reassure them that they are still members of your child's family and that, as such, you intend to do everything you can to maintain their relationship with your child(ren).

♦ If all else fails, talk to your ex. He knows his parents better than you and might be able to help.

Grandparents have their say

♦♦ *We were so relieved when our daughter's marriage came to an end that we weren't at all worried about her being a single parent. We just hoped that she could make a happy life for herself and Thomas after all she'd been through. It's not really in Louise's nature to ask for help, but obviously she needed it and we were very happy to give it, especially because it meant we got to see a lot of Thomas, which was a blessing and a delight to all of us (myself, my own mum and my husband).* ♦♦

June and Patrick

♦♦ *I sometimes felt frustrated by my daughter's unwillingness to take advice, especially when she was really struggling, but eventually I learnt that if I kept my mouth shut, she came to me for help and that worked a lot better.* ♦♦

Bob

♦♦ *Our main concern was the emotional effect the split would have on the kids and our daughter. We'd felt she would be better off without her husband, who was useless, to say the least, but we worried that it would be hard on the kids, and were concerned about the financial position they would be in and where they were going to live. Our daughter was too proud to ask for financial help, and was reluctant to accept when it was offered. She was more able to ask for practical help, such as looking after the girls when necessary, which we were really happy to do. We were more than happy to give any support she wanted or needed, but I don't think she ever really believed that. It's not until your own kids grow up that you realise you never stop being their parents. I liked being in a position to help my daughter – to be her mum.* ♦♦

Toni

♦♦ *Our grandson has been through a lot emotionally in his young life and we think he has handled it all admirably. His parents split up when he was little, then shortly afterwards a stepfather and three stepsisters moved in, two of whom he no longer sees as they moved back to their mum's. He also has a tricky on-off relationship with his dad, and while he feels loyal to his mum, he doesn't always agree with her decisions. Luckily, he's always had the love of his mum, his grandparents (on both sides) and great-grandmothers, so I hope he has no doubts on that score anyway.* ♦♦

Paula and Rod

♦♦ *My eldest granddaughter's very sociable and strong-minded. She has a mature assessment of her father's failings and came to her own conclusions about him, eventually deciding not to see him at all once she was 16. Her sister is a more anxious child and worries a lot. She likes to please and will avoid confrontation at all costs. She went through a period when she was very angry – I think her tantrums and rages used to frighten her a bit. She is able to show affection now, has developed a great sense of humour and is quite realistic about her father's limitations. I'm deeply proud of both girls and their mother.* ♦♦

Stanley

Social life

By social life, I mean interacting with our peers, connecting with our old friends, and meeting new people, whether it's down the pub, at yours or a friend's house, or on a picnic in the park. This is not to be confused with our romantic life. Although a good social life can be a means to that particular end, it's also an end unto itself. Love, as most of us know, can come and go, but a good circle of friends, if regularly tended, is for life and is therefore invaluable to a good sense of security and belonging – especially if family doesn't provide it.

Ask a single parent to describe their social life and the response you're likely to get is, 'What social life?' Having fun doesn't usually register very high on the list of priorities we're forced to make when time, money and energy are limited, but I believe it's essential to maintain or create as active a social life as possible. I'm talking about friendship, interaction with social groups, meeting new people, flirting and generally hanging out with other grown-ups outside of a work context.

Not being in a romantic partnership can leave us feeling socially isolated in a world of seemingly endless happy couples. Being the only unaccompanied person at a dinner party, getting invitations with '+ guest' next to your name, or wanting to punch the very next person who asks how your love life is going can get pretty tiresome, but there are upsides to being single – if we're willing to make the effort. In fact, it's often harder to maintain a good social life while in a relationship.

Maggie, a single mum with two children, had been very outgoing in the early days of her marriage, but had become totally isolated by the end of it. 'My husband was very insecure about me having any life of my own. I used to go out for an occasional glass of wine with the girls, but over the years he became more and more possessive of my time. I used to encourage

PHONE A FRIEND

Not having a partner means there's no one at home to ask, 'How's your day been?' It might not sound like a big deal, but it's this conversation that gives us a chance to process the day: what was good, what was bad. It's where we get a pat on the back and advice if we want it (and sometimes when we don't). It's like a mini-therapy session that keeps things in perspective and helps to put the day we've just had to bed, so we can relax and prepare for the one ahead. Being single's not a good reason to skip this routine. Get a hands-free headset and call someone who'll be up for a good moan exchange while you're making tea.

him to go out with his friends, but he said he didn't want to. He couldn't understand why I needed time away from him and the kids occasionally, and made such a fuss that in the end it was easier to just stop going out.'

Being single offers us a fantastic opportunity not just to reconnect with old friends, but to get out there and discover a few new ones too.

Getting back on the horse

Even if you're not heartbroken from your last relationship, going out socially can feel scary for loads of reasons. First, we tend to define ourselves as one half of a couple, so when our other half is removed, it leaves us feeling like half a person. It takes a while to remember how to act in social situations and to find our confident, witty self all over again. The first few times can feel awful. I remember spending one dinner party counting the minutes till I'd be able to leave without appearing rude. I didn't seem to have anything to say to anyone, and no one seemed to be even trying to talk to me. They were all couples who knew each other very well, but I knew only the hostess, and as she was busy delivering courses, I was left fumbling my napkin in my lap, feeling like the biggest Billy-no-mates in the land. If I could go back and visit myself on that night right now, I'd point out to myself that just because my friend was busy and preoccupied didn't mean she wasn't available for a private hug in the kitchen and a word of reassurance. I'd merely lost my social confidence, but it made me feel like a hopeless leper.

A FRIEND IN NEED...

If you're going to attend dinner parties made up of couples and you're feeling a tad self-conscious, take a pal. Not only will they save you from feeling like the odd one out, but they'll help to avoid that potentially dark moment at the end when you have to leave alone and don't have anyone to do the post-mortem gossip with.

Who am I?

My uncomfortable dinner party experience was shortly after my long-term partner had moved out of our home and taken all his belongings. As I looked around at what was left, I realised I had almost nothing that represented the last five years of my life. I'd stopped growing my own sense of identity. My CD collection stopped at 1997; the books that lined the shelves were those I'd had at college; my squash racket had collected dust; and my wardrobe said more about my ex's tastes than my own. Most of the friends we saw regularly had been his because he didn't like mine. Had I just been shadowing his life? I could have given you every detail of my son's likes and dislikes, and my ex's, but it had been such a long time since I'd really focused on me that I didn't have a clue what I wanted to hear, watch, wear, buy, see or do.

It can feel hard to remember that we ever existed without children or a partner, but we did, and when we did we had, among other things, a strong sense of our own identity, which was revealed in the clothes we wore, the music we listened to, where we went and with whom. Even if we didn't know who we were, we knew who we aspired to be. It's easy to lose ourselves in the midst of parenthood and partnership. Being single gives us the chance to establish the kind of social life *we* want without having to consider a partner's needs, so when we find ourselves involved again, we'll know if we're compromising too much.

Discover your personal profile

Make a list of all the things you really enjoy doing. Include as many activities as you can think of: the music you like to listen to, films you like to watch, restaurants you prefer to eat in, what kind of TV programmes you enjoy. Think about the kind of nights out you want to have and with whom. Are there any hobbies or one-off activities you've always wanted to try? What constitutes 'fun' for you, and how much of it do you need?

If you find it hard to answer these questions, you're probably out of touch with your needs. Stick your list on the wall and commit to rediscovering yourself. Add at least one new 'like' to the list every day, even if it's just a tune you heard on the radio. That way, when someone asks what you like to do when you're not busy being a parent, you'll know what to say.

Social life? Hah!

Some of you might think that being a single parent is a good excuse not to have to take the scary leap back into the social loop. The fact that Paul was a single parent of three left him pretty confident that his lack of social life was unchallenge-able, and he made a pretty good case against being able to do anything to change it. He came to me as a client desperate for help with managing his three daughters, all under 11, who had moved in with him a year earlier when his ex-wife's job meant she had to move to a different city. Rather than put them through the trauma of changing schools, he decided to take on the mantle of main carer. When I asked him about his social life, he threw back his head and laughed loudly and bitterly. He leaned forward in his chair and recounted his day:

> My alarm goes off at 6 a.m. I get the kids up, dressed, fed and to their breakfast club for 7.15 so I can be at work for 8.30, where I stay until 6 p.m. I pick them up from after-school club, feed, bathe and listen to them. Then I put the two little ones to bed with a story and help the eldest with her homework before she goes to bed too. Then, if I'm lucky, once I've washed up, made the packed lunches, taken one load of washing out to dry, put another one in and ironed myself a shirt for the morning, I might have enough energy to watch a bit of mindless telly.

The weekends didn't sound much better.

> Meeting all the kids' social engagements, clubs and hobbies is a military operation. Take last Saturday. Jenny has to be at ballet for 10 a.m. and Charlotte's gymnastic club starts 20 minutes later across town, so it's always tight and there are no contingencies

for needing the loo (Jenny) or forgetting a bit of kit (Charlotte).
They were both late, which meant I didn't have time to buy Har-
riet the new shoes I'd promised she could wear to her friend's
birthday party that afternoon. She complained all the way there,
despite the fact that I had performed a minor miracle by remem-
bering not only to buy a gift for her to take, but by wrapping it
up too. We were still in the supermarket doing the weekly shop
at 7 p.m. that night.

Paul had barely drawn breath the whole time he'd been talk-ing. I asked him how he felt and he said, 'Exhausted.' Some-thing was going to give; it was only a question of which would go first, his health or his sanity.

When I asked about his support mechanisms, it turned out that he had a lot. His parents were willing to help out and were 'always offering', as were his former in-laws, his brother's wife and the next-door neighbour. I was baffled. Why didn't he avail himself of it more often – or at all? The short version was that he felt no one had believed he could pull it off. When he first told his family, friends and colleagues that his kids were coming to live with him, he felt a lot of opposition, which he thought was sexist. No one had suggested his wife wouldn't be able to cope on her own, so why was everyone pulling a face at the idea of him doing the same job? He set out to prove every-one wrong, and in doing so, almost proved everyone right.

SAFETY IN NUMBERS

If you're not interested in 'meeting someone', hang out with couples. Single friends can be all about finding the next man or woman, so if you're not up for that, avoid fellow singles, or you're in for some long evenings acting as a bored passenger on someone else's lurve train!

Pride's a patsy

They say that pride comes before a fall, but in my experience, it comes after one. Pride is the cloak we use to cover it up. Haughtiness, defensiveness and perfectionism are characteristics of the proud. As a teenage mum, I was painfully aware that I was not expected to cope very well. When my son was born, I remember how my midwives, doctors at the hospital, other mums and my GP all made me feel as though failing was a foregone conclusion. It made me furious, so I decided to prove that I could do it without anyone's help, and I managed, but by the time my son was almost three, I was tearing my hair out. It was like being terribly thirsty but too proud to sip from the well of support. What it meant was that when I did finally come across someone I trusted to help, and raised that cup to my lips, I couldn't stop myself from drinking it dry.

Aileen was 16 years old when she agreed to babysit my son during her summer holidays. As the eldest of six, she'd grown up taking care of her younger siblings, so she was well qualified, and besides that, my toddler son thought she was 'bwillyant'. For the first time in his life I had some real freedom and it went straight to my head. I had my first love affair since his father and I split up, took on more work (to pay Aileen), went out socially on my nights off, and before I knew it, my babysitter was a semi-reluctant, full-time nanny. I knew it wasn't right. Deep down I felt bad for abusing Aileen's natural sense of generosity, but the guilt I felt in greedily buying up her entire summer holiday was cancelled out by the intoxicating allure of rediscovering my Self. I rushed most of our conversations to avoid giving her the space to complain about how much she was doing, and paid her over the average in the hope that she would feel compensated. It wasn't until she stopped returning my calls that I realised I'd pushed my luck too far.

Do me a favour!

♦♦ *I have a friend that I hate asking favours from because I swear she keeps a little book that lists everything she has ever done for anyone. It's as though her favours are money and she wants every penny paying back with interest. Except if she does have a little book, she forgets to write in the times when people do pay her back, or when she owes someone else. It does my head in, but our kids are best friends and it would just be so nice if things could be free and easy.* ♦♦

The thing you have to check out is whether her favour is a 'gift' or a 'deal'. A gift is something given in pleasure with a free heart and no conditions. A deal, on the other hand, is an agreement, arrangement or transaction. Problems occur precisely because it isn't always clear which is which when we accept an offer of help. Next time she 'offers' to help you or agrees to do a favour, try saying this: 'Is this a gift or a deal? If it's a deal, that's OK by me, but I need you to let me know what you expect in return before I agree to shake on it.' That will put the cat among the pigeons. The same goes for when she asks a favour from you. Say: 'I just want you to know that this is a gift, and as far as I'm concerned, you owe me nothing in return.' Or: 'If I do this thing for you, can I expect that you will do the same for me if I need you to?' If that doesn't nail the message, get a little book of your own!

You don't get to choose your family...

...but you do get to choose your friends. If you're one of those single parents who doesn't have access to practical and or emotional family support, friends are the next best thing, and in some cases they're better because they don't come with a lifetime's historical baggage. Friends are essential ingredients to well-being. Josie, who'd been a young single mum, never doubted it. 'They're vital. Mine have been and still are a real network of support and comfort. My friends don't worry about me like my parents do; they advise and encourage without judging me or making me feel useless. We swap complaints, pass the ice cream and toast ourselves with vats of red wine for being brilliant mums, even when we feel rubbish.'

Andrea, however, had moved around a lot and didn't have that hardcore network of old friends to fall back on after the sudden death of her husband left her alone with their eight-year-old daughter. She had to make do with her mum.

She was great, and I feel terrible for saying anything bad about her. She was really there for me, but she wasn't my friend; she was my mum, and always had the upper hand. When me and my brother were kids, she was like this perfect housewife. Everything was spotless, the tea was never late on the table for my dad, she could nearly always help with our homework, and we thought all kitchens smelt of freshly baked something. I'd never share my fears or my failings with her because I already felt as though I'd never measure up to her standards. It wasn't until I started a course at an adult learning centre, where I met and befriended other mums, that I realised just how much I'd allowed my mother's perfectionism to infect the way I felt about myself as a mum. These days, if I feel like a bad parent because I haven't washed up for three days, my friends laugh

and remind me that while I might be slack about housework,
I have a fantastic relationship with a daughter who trusts
that I love her for who she is and not how perfect she can be.

Choose your mirror

Other people are our mirrors; they reflect us in different ways depending on how they experience us. The more people we invite into our world, the more angles we see ourselves from. Write down the names of the most prominent people in your life, then next to each one describe how you see yourself reflected in them. If a friend reflects back to you that you are unreliable, unmotivated and a bit rubbish, ask yourself why you're keeping that person around. I hear a lot that we shouldn't care about what people think of us, but that's nonsense. We want to see ourselves reflected well in the eyes of the people that count. It's only when you find yourself trying to get approval from random strangers that there might be an issue.

When you're a child the only mirror you have to judge and compare yourself against is your family mirror. Families have a tendency to attach labels to each other, which you then feel you have to try and live up to or escape from. Are you living with a label your family gave you? Are you the 'clever one' or the 'spoilt one' or the 'bad one'? This is reason alone to have as many good friendships as you can find time for because their reflection of you won't be tainted with family history. Find mirrors that reflect back the things you like about yourself.

Feeling beholden

Indebtedness is a poison that eats away at confidence, entitlement, self-esteem and pride (sense of worth). It's the assumption that we owe someone something we can't pay. It shows up with teachers, friends, the parents of your children's friends, babysitters, nannies, neighbours and colleagues – basically anyone you have ever asked to go out of their way to accommodate the fact that no matter how hard you try, there is only one of you and you cannot be in two places at the same time. Asking family for help is hard enough, but having to rely on the patience and generosity of non-related friends and sometimes relative strangers is an exercise in abject humility. Asking for favours can feel like using a credit card: you know there's a limit to what you can have and that it's an expensive way to get what you need, so you try to save it for emergencies, but for single parents, those emergencies can feel never-ending. You know that repaying the minimum isn't actually clearing the debt – it's just stopping you from being penalised, but you can only afford the minimum, so it has to do.

We hate the feeling of being in debt, so we live in denial of it and don't open the monthly statements, hoping that what we're not looking at can't hurt us. But of course it does. It makes us feel anxious, it diminishes our sense of worth and, worst of all, it makes us feel ashamed. In the end we do everything we can to avoid the person we feel indebted to, which can mean losing that support for good.

Gratitude is the antidote

A friendship is like a joint bank account: you're both equally responsible for its upkeep, which means making regular deposits and agreeing on withdrawals to make sure that you're not overdrawing. The balances are reconciled every month because our spending behaviour ebbs and flows from week to week. One person might have a lot to give at the beginning of the month, but have a serious dip in the middle, and need a large withdrawal. As long as the other partner can cover for this till they get back on their feet, the account will remain buoyant. A really good friendship can withstand balancing the account every three months because it's the overall behaviour that makes us feel we're in an equal relationship, not the minute to minute of asking favours and paying them back.

Fran didn't find it easy to ask for help from friends back when her kids were still at school, but as she had limited access to family, she had no choice. While her pals seemed more than happy to help out, she couldn't help but feel beholden to them for it. She recognised the creeping rot of indebtedness setting in, especially over the summer holidays when she had to make a lot more withdrawals than deposits.

*My friends were great, but I hated asking them for help because I knew I couldn't reciprocate. Most of them had kids of a similar age to mine, but they had partners, which meant they were more flexible than I could be. **They** didn't have an issue with the imbalance – **I** did. I needed to pay them back to stop me feeling like a local charity case. The problem was that I couldn't pick their kids up from school or take care of them when they were ill. I was a working single mum.*

'What do I have to offer?' I wailed one day at a friend. She gave me a hug and said, 'Food'. She told me how much they all loved my cooking, and a dinner party every now and then would more than compensate for their support. I thought she was just being kind, but I invited them round for dinner anyway and it made me feel great. I was saying thank you in a way they really appreciated, and it opened up a whole new

*social aspect to my life. We started a dinner circuit. I used to
take the kids with me when they were little. They'd fall asleep
on my friends' sofas, and when it was time to go home I'd
wrap them in blankets and bundle them into the car. Or we'd
socialise early and go home early. I'd thought payback had to
be favour for favour. Once I realised that gratitude could be
paid in kind, indebtedness was no longer an issue.*

Groups, clubs, coffee mornings and other nightmares

When single parents complain to me of feeling isolated or lonely
I regularly suggest attending parent and child groups, but this
is often met with an expression of distaste or disgust. 'I hardly
see myself as a member of a coffee morning, do you?' asked
one mum who sported a pink Mohican haircut. And then there
was Paul's response: 'Yeah, right, me and six women talking
about sore nipples and fake tan? I don't think so, thanks.'

Angie felt sure she wouldn't fit in either: 'They'll all be
married and have big houses and cars, and I'll have nothing in
common with any of them.' Liz said she would love to have the
support of a mothers' group, but her relationship had knocked
all the confidence out of her. 'I just wouldn't know what to
say.' Then there are those who think it's downright uncool.
Jean was a hip young woman who worked in television and
saw mums' groups as something her own mother would have
done, not something she could ever see herself doing, which is
what makes her an interesting advocate for them.

*I'd just moved lock, stock and barrel from Scotland to London
for work when I discovered I was nine weeks pregnant from
a one-night stand I only vaguely remembered having. I'd left
behind all my friends and, more importantly, four supportive*

*sisters. I knew a few people in London, but none I'd call friends. Not having anyone to share my pregnancy with made it a lonely experience, but it didn't prepare me for the feelings of hopeless isolation I felt after I had my daughter. I'd taken extended maternity leave and was desperate for friends. I would strike up conversations with other mums (though not dads in case they thought I was hitting on them) whenever I came across them – in parks, supermarkets and doctors' waiting rooms. My health visitor had suggested a local mothers' group, and while I was desperate, I wasn't sure if I was **that** desperate. I imagined myself sitting in a room with a group of women clutching small babies and discussing feeding rituals, and it didn't exactly whet my appetite. I was sure I'd hate it, but I decided to go, just to see what it was like. Sure enough, I found myself sitting in a room with a group of women, clutching screaming babies and discussing feeding rituals. And it felt great! It was exactly what I needed.*

The group was a lifeline for Jean, and a real eye-opener.

Some of us were single, others married; some worked, while others stayed at home; some were first-time mums, others had kids already, but it was the similarities that bonded us, and for the first time in my life the differences were less important.

We shared, helped, talked, cared for and looked out for each other and our babies. In their company it was OK to panic, fuss, moan, cry and freak out. Our screaming babies all started reception class earlier this year, and if I hadn't had my friends to compare notes with, I might have thought I was odd for sobbing my heart out at the school gates after my daughter skipped out of sight on her first day without even glancing back. We've watched each other's children grow from babies to little people. They sleep over at each other's houses. They're best friends. They squabble and they love each other like siblings. They're a lot like us.

A great friendship is like a great marriage, but without the sex. Take the sex out of a romantic relationship and you're left with just the relationship. While we seem reasonably accepting of the fact that good marriages require hard work, commitment, loyalty and understanding, we think friendships should just be there for us when we need them without giving a thought as to what they might need from us. Mostly we don't live with our friends, and because we don't usually expect them to 'make us happy' as we do our partners, there's less in the way of expectation, but that doesn't mean we get to relax entirely. Good friendships require all the things that good partnerships do.

Work life

Work is the fourth leg on our table of stability. It's the one that connects us to the outside world and is the yardstick we use to measure our growth, success, achievement and fulfilment. It supplies the means to a higher standard of living, and sets a benchmark for our children's future expectations of themselves.

GET REAL

While Internet chatrooms are great ways to pass the time, catch up with new parenting techniques, meet people and have a good old moan, they should not be mistaken for *real* human contact. They're just a temporary substitute. Don't get lulled into thinking you're having a great social life if you never leave your living room. Hibernation is for polar bears, not brave, vital defenders of the next generation!

For single parents who work – full or part time, self-employed or PAYE, earning lots of money or a little – the issues surrounding the work–life balance are complicated, emotionally challenging and physically exhausting, which is why it's often this area of life that causes the most stress. We work because we want the best for our kids, yet it's our job that gets in the way of our being the parents we want to be. Work can leave us too tired physically or mentally to help with homework, laugh at knock-knock jokes, stand up to a teenager, or cook a nutritious dinner at the end of the day. At the weekends we can feel resentful having to ferry the kids to their various activities and do household chores instead of nestling into the sofa and working our way through a DVD boxed set or the Sunday papers. And if we choose to go part time and take the hit financially, we might also be saying goodbye to promotions, and have to deal with not being taken seriously by our bosses and colleagues in a competitive workplace where the macho mantra is 'S/he who works longest (but not necessarily hardest) wins'.

Daddy, you're fired!

✦✦ I feel really guilty about the fact that I put more into my job than I do my children, and that a lot of the time I enjoy it more than being a parent. I adore my kids, but the days I spend at home can drag, and I look forward to going back to work. I feel like a terrible father. ✦✦

At work we get feedback, companionship, stimulation and other adult stuff, such as flirting, risqué jokes and clever conversation. Parenting is repetitive, often boring, and is generally a one-way street. We give, they take. Everyone needs different types of stimulation, and there's a limit to how much toddler telly anyone can handle before imploding. We tend to perform more reliably in our paid jobs because there's a risk of being fired if we don't. If our kids could fire us from being their parents (and they'd almost certainly have just cause: laziness, inconsistency, poor attention to detail, erratic behaviour and failure to meet conditions of contract), we'd probably make more effort.

Listen to your instincts. They're telling you that you're not trying hard enough at home. Stop wasting time feeling guilty, and instead plan some activities with the kids. If you're bored, the chances are they are too. Luckily for us, they don't have any point of comparison, so we can tell them we're the best parents ever and they won't know any better!

Public opinion on mums…

The two things to remember about public opinion is that it changes all the time and that you can't win. In the work versus kids debate I've seen women being slated in the press all my life. I remember newspaper stories in the late 1970s asking whether women who 'put their careers first' were unmaternal, butch, over-ambitious and self-serving. Now we put off having kids until the last possible moment so that we can compete in the workplace, and we're suffering for that too. Don't think you can get away with it by not having a career, because then you're 'letting the side down', unless you have a partner to take care of the finances, in which case you're the perfect mother: one who sacrifices her professional dreams for her kids. If, however, it's at the expense of the state, opinion suddenly gets much less generous, and you're pressed to get any old job, no matter how low paid or humble, to support your kids. Oh, and if you do get that job, watch out for the low-flying attacks about unsociable adolescent behaviour being a consequence of parents who were never at home for their kids.

Public opinion on dads...

Men who become full-time dads, financially independent or not, often have to face outrageous and outdated sexist attitudes. Men who break rank are often treated with suspicion and derision. I remember an old friend of mine, Jonathon, telling me how his job used to mean he was away from home for days at a time, so when his long-term partner left him, he left his job. 'My partner had been full-time carer to our eldest son, who is autistic. I didn't want to put him in the care of strangers, so I decided to look after him and his sisters myself, full time. My friends were really supportive, but new people are a different story. Blokes ask twice what I do, as if they can't believe their ears the first time, and women either go all gooey, like I'm some kind of hero, or eye me suspiciously, as if I might be looking for a mother for my kids.'

Full time – full on

Whoever coined the phrase 'race against time' was probably a single parent with a full-time job. It starts with the morning rush to get the kids to school on time so that you can be at work on time so that you can leave on time to ensure that you'll be on time to pick them up again. Then you feed them and fight to get them into bed on time so they'll get up in time to start the whole thing again in the morning. Then you have to stomach the emotional wrangling involved in dividing your time and energy between kids demanding attention as proof of love and employers demanding attendance as proof of commitment. You're just getting into the swing of it when school breaks up for yet another holiday and everything goes to pot.

In your spare time (ha!) you might pick up a newspaper and read about those undeserving parents who 'fob' their kids off to nannies, nurseries and after-school clubs while they selfishly gad about in full-time work just so they can pay for those important little luxuries, such as a cone with a flake when the ice cream van comes round. Throw in a few office politics, some distinctly unequal opportunities and a bit of workplace prejudice and it's a wonder that any parent attempts full-time work.

No choice?

♦♦ *My girls were three and five when I left my husband. I had to work full time because their father refused to pay a penny in maintenance. I couldn't stand by and watch my children go without while I waited for the CSA to take action against him, so I extended my hours. It meant that the girls had to go to an after-school club, which they hated, but I had no choice. I'd rather work part time because I have more energy for the girls, but I refuse to make them suffer just because their dad is so irresponsible.* ♦♦

Ask yourself honestly, are you working full time just to prove a point to your ex, or do you genuinely think it's the right thing for your family? Is it possible that maybe your time and energy might be more valuable to the girls than the things you can buy, at least for now? Telling yourself you've no choice is making you feel forced to act against your will, and there's no way to feel OK about that. You're not powerless. Circumstances may force your hand sometimes, but ultimately you always have a choice. Make a decision based entirely on what you want to do, and feel good about it. The great thing about being the boss of your life rather than a victim of it is that you get to take the credit when it all goes right.

Work pays

While money can't buy happiness directly, it can certainly relieve some of the stress and give us a break from our unhappiness. Having enough to run a car, take holidays, have days out, employ babysitters, pay for ballet lessons and buy football boots makes all the difference to our daily sense of well-being. Working to earn the means to treat yourself and your kids is an extremely satisfying experience and shouldn't be underestimated. Money is power whether we think it should be or not. With money, we have more control over what we do than when we have none. Being skint is an awful feeling. I lived on benefits for years, and will never forget how powerless I felt over my life. I couldn't go anywhere or do anything that cost money, no matter how little, because every penny was accounted for. Even so, it wasn't the thought of having money that eventually inspired me to take a leap of faith and get a job. It was the need for fresh experiences.

Bringing up kids alone is a permanent full-time job, where full time means all the time. As the sole employee, there's no one to take over when you feel you just can't do it any more. There are no appraisals or promotions, so you never know if you're doing a good job, and the rewards aren't always easy to see. It's not thankless, though no one does thank you, preferring instead to complain about what you're getting wrong, while what you get right passes by unnoticed. It's not surprising that some of us want a second job, one that appreciates our efforts by presenting us with a wage packet, a pat on the back every now and then, *and* holiday pay.

> ♦♦ *Money can't buy you happiness, but it does bring you a more pleasant form of misery.* ♦♦
> Spike Milligan

Case: Juliet and Lily

Juliet was 37 and single when her daughter was born. She'd worked all her life and was really looking forward to being a full-time mother. She'd managed to save enough money to allow her to be a stay-at-home mum until her daughter was three, but after two years she'd had enough.

'I felt like my brain was melting. All the things that I used to be great at – my negotiating skills, my three languages, my killer backhand and my ability to drink any man under the table – were all suddenly meaningless. I felt like I was losing myself, so I went back to work part time until Lily went to school, then I went full time. I suffer constantly with split loyalties and guilt, but overall I believe we're both better off because I'm a happier mum when I'm fulfilled intellectually.'

When work's not working

While work can be great in many ways, it can also be a source of utter misery. It can act as a drain on our time and energy, taking more than it gives and leaving us resentful and frustrated. It can challenge us in ways we don't want to be challenged, and when there's not another adult at home to discuss our frustrations with, we can end up taking them out on the people we look to for support or, even worse, our kids. If we're unhappy at work, we need to decide whether to try to resolve the problems or to walk away because staying in a bad job is every bit as destructive as staying in a bad relationship. I believe that work is an essential ingredient to happiness, but it has to be the right work, and, just like the right relationship, we don't always find it first time; and even when we do, it still requires regular maintenance to keep things running smoothly.

When work is working, we feel good about ourselves. We know who we are and where we're going. It improves our confidence and raises our self-esteem so that we feel we could conquer anything. If that's not how your job makes you feel at least some of the time, you might want to think about changing it or taking a break from it to give yourself time to work out what you want or how to make your work life better. Use the exercise below as a starting point.

The work–life balance

1 Imagine your life is a pie. Draw a circle and divide it into slices that represent how much time you spend on each of the following in an average week.

- ◆ At work (include travelling time)
- ◆ Taking care of the kids' needs
- ◆ Spending real quality time with the kids
- ◆ Socialising with/talking to friends
- ◆ Seeing family
- ◆ Spending time with a lover
- ◆ You time

2 Looking at how your pie is divided, ask yourself the following questions.

- ◆ Are there any surprises?
- ◆ Are you happy with the way you're spending your time?
- ◆ Are there any changes you would like to make?
- ◆ If yes, what's stopping you?

3 Using a different-coloured pen, draw new lines on the chart that represent how you would like the divisions to be, and decide what you can do differently to make room for the changes.

How to make home work better

Make time! The more we do something, the better and more proficient we get at doing it and the less time it takes to do. Implement routines wherever you can. They'll feel awkward at first, but they will eventually *save* time.

Commit to having one weekend day to relax and have fun as a family. This means that if you haven't done the shopping, washing, cleaning or homework, it stays undone. Making your family an absolute priority one day a week will help you to feel like you're doing your job at home as well as at work.

Get the shopping delivered. Quite a few of the major supermarkets have virtual aisles, so you can do your weekly shop online and they'll deliver it for a few quid. How much is that two hours worth to you?

Go to bed. It's tempting when you work all day and parent all evening to stay up late into the night just to feel as though you've had some 'you' time, but it's a self-defeating plan. You need your energy, and that comes from rest.

Don't cook – cater. Make batches of freezable nutritious foods, such as vegetable stew, corned beef hash, hearty soups and bolognese sauce, so that when you're whacked and can't be bothered to cook, you don't always end up serving micro-waved burgers and chips and feeling guilty later on.

Get the kids involved in the domestic chores, but make it fun. Try having different music for different tasks, such as hanging out the washing, and see if you can get everything pegged up before it ends. Kids hate chores because they take them away from the action, but if the chores are where the action's at, they'll want to join in.

How to make work, work better

Keep positive. Psychologically speaking, we have a lot of control over how someone responds to something we say – it's the way we say it. For example, deliver the news that your child is ill and you can't find a sitter in a matter-of-fact way, and follow this up with a plan of action. Your boss is much less likely to think of it as a problem if you don't present it as one.

Don't apologise for being a single parent. It gives the impression that there's something to be sorry for, and there just isn't. Take the lead, hold your head high and challenge anyone to suggest anything differently – they won't.

Under-promise and over-deliver. We hate being let down, so keep expectations reasonable by keeping the boss and colleagues in the picture. Remember that the expectations we have of ourselves are usually much higher than others have of us.

Be upfront about the limitations that being a single parent place on you and do what you can well, rather than attempt to do more than your circumstances make possible and fail.

Try to find creative solutions to the problems that being a single parent can impose on your career, and talk to other parents at work about the issues. Whether they're lone parents or not, they'll be facing similar issues, and pooling ideas might inspire new ones about how to confront them.

Don't tolerate prejudice. A recent report suggested that single mothers receive the most prejudice in the workplace, so stand up for yourself by knowing your rights and not being afraid to assert them.

All or nothing

Don't fall into the trap of thinking that stopping work altogether is the answer. Not working has its own special brand of stress for two reasons. First, the fact that unpaid work isn't rewarded with the same respect as a job that earns hard cash (as anyone who's been a housewife or househusband knows only too well) means that it's hard to hold on to a sense of our own value. Second, when the work–life balance is tipped too much the other way, we can find ourselves not knowing what to do with our time. Once you're done with the housework and domestic chores, you can easily find yourself drumming your fingers, waiting for 3.30, when you can pick up your little distractions once more. In addition, not working can also leave us feeling a bit exiled from the world around us.

These days, when meeting new people, you're more likely to hear, 'What do you do?' than 'How do you do'. I recently overheard a woman being asked just that at a friend's barbecue. 'Nothing, I'm just a mum,' she replied with a slight shrug. She completely wrote herself off. A few minutes later the woman slipped away and I went over to say hi. Sara was a single mum to three boys who were with their father for the weekend. 'Normally I'd be running around trying to stop them from getting ketchup over everyone. I'm always moaning that I don't get time for a life because of the kids, but now I don't know what to do with myself.' Sara had been an events organiser, which she managed to combine with being a wife and mother just fine until her husband left her for someone else. The stress of maintaining a career, looking after three heartbroken children and going through an acrimonious divorce brought her close to a breakdown. 'Something had to go. It was between my sanity, my kids and my job, so the job went, but sometimes I think a part of me went with it. I used to be really confident, and now I feel like a social leper.'

Sara, like a lot of people with successful careers, felt she lost her identity along with her job. She's a classic example of the all or nothing, black and white thinking we can slip into. Just because she couldn't meet the demands of *that* job and be the mum she wanted to be at *that* time didn't mean she'd have to resign herself to the single focus of being purely a mother, letting go of all she had worked hard to achieve for the rest of their childhoods. Her experience of failing to meet all the demands placed upon her had badly knocked her confidence and she'd begun to recede into herself, feeling more and more estranged from the world.

Sara's situation was not that different from my own. Until my son went to school, I claimed Income Support rather than work in a job that would pay little and offer even less in the way of self-esteem. I wasn't qualified to do anything that would pay enough to make full-time work worth my while. Once I'd paid for childcare, travel to work, prescriptions, dental care, school lunches, council tax and rent, I'd probably be worse off – a fact that made me feel trapped and desperately unhappy. At that time, you were allowed to earn £15 a week without affecting your Income Support, so I took a lunchtime job serving behind the counter in a fish and chip shop. I was embarrassed at first; I felt it was beneath me, but the extra cash, measly as it was, meant that I could run a car, which made all the difference to my life. Having to chat to different people every day and work alongside my boss, who was a bright, interesting man, slowly built up my confidence without me noticing. Before long I applied for a position as an outreach worker that paid only the same as my benefits plus chippy wage, but gave me an invaluable sense of the possibilities. In that same year I started my diploma in psychotherapy and hypnosis, and wrote a novel that was later published. I couldn't have known it at the time, but that little part-time job formed the basis of what would eventually grow into what I'm proud to call my career.

Returning to work

A couple of years ago I worked on a double episode of Trevor MacDonald's *The Tonight Show*. It focused on the lives of two single mums who'd been out of work since they'd become parents four and seven years earlier. Both mums said they desperately wanted to go back to work, but even if they managed to find a job that would accommodate the school run, how would they deal with the school holidays? What would happen when they needed time off to look after sick children? And would the work pay enough to make it worth their while? They had a million reasonable concerns, but when it came down to it, the biggest block was a debilitating lack of self-belief. Mum 'A' had been a supervising croupier in charge of a team on a cruise liner, and Mum 'B' had travelled the world as a holiday rep. These two once-worldly women both now found the thought of interviewing for a job terrifying. They'd lost all their confidence, and were unwittingly using their children as an excuse not to step out into the world and risk being rejected by it. Going back to work after being out of the loop for a considerable time can be a very scary challenge.

Rebuilding confidence

If you hear your internal voice saying 'I can't', it means 'I'm too scared to try'. There's nothing wrong with feeling afraid, but if you can work out exactly what it is you're afraid of, you've a better chance of getting back in control of your life. There's a famous self-help book by Susan Jeffers called *Feel the Fear and Do it Anyway* (Vermilion, 2007), and while the lessons of the book escape me now, the title has always stuck fast. It reminds us that fear is just a feeling, not a fact, and feelings can be overcome with patience and understanding.

Most of our fears are just beneath our conscious awareness, so we have to investigate them properly. Whether your fear is of going back to work, leaving work, changing jobs, asking for a pay rise, challenging prejudice, saying no, demanding your rights, or dealing with bullies, you will be telling yourself a story that begins with your daring to challenge the situation and ends in disaster. This process happens so fast in your brain that you barely register it happening at all consciously, but unconsciously you are absorbing those thoughts as facts.

Here's an example of that thought process, which I call the 'If…then' story.

If I apply for a job, then I risk not getting it. If I don't get it, then I'll have to apply for another, and if I don't get that either, then I'll know I'm not good enough. If I'm not good enough, then I might as well not bother trying, which means I'll never have a job, and if I never work again, then I'll never have any money or pride. If I have no pride, then people will think I'm worthless, and if I'm worthless, then no one will want me, and if no one wants me, then I'll be alone for ever.

Your answer to the dilemma – delivered faster than the speed of light – is therefore: if I apply for that job, then I'll be alone for ever.

What 'If…then' stories might you be telling yourself? Think about this, then try telling yourself a positive story about what might happen, and see if you feel differently. For example:

If I apply for that job and get it, then I'll feel great about myself, and if that happens, then my confidence will grow, and if I feel confident, then I'll do well, and if I do well, then I'll get a promotion that will pay more money, and if I get paid more, then I'll be able to take the kids on holiday, and if I can do that, then we'll get time to bond as family, and if we're bonded, then we'll always be close, and if we're always close, then I'll never be alone.

Even though this is an equally far-fetched story, it's more likely to inspire confidence and optimism than the other version. If you're going to tell yourself a story at all, why on earth wouldn't you make it a good one?

Case: Andrea

Andrea made the decision not to work based on her own childhood experience, which she wanted to replicate.

> *There was never a time when I came in from school and there wasn't a nice smell coming from the kitchen and a jolly 'Hello, how was school today?' My mum was always there. I wanted my children to take me for granted in the same way, but unlike my mum, who was a child of the '50s and, as such, had a whole network of other women also at home to lean on, not to mention my dad bringing home the bacon, I was very isolated. And then there was the matter of the 'bacon'. If I was staying at home to 'bake cookies', who was going to pay for the ingredients? As a single parent, if I wanted to be time-rich, I was going to have to accept being pocket poor, and that was the gloomiest thing of all. With no money, no mates to hang out with in the day, and no man coming home at night, I didn't feel much like baking cookies or smiling.*

Andrea did the next best thing: she enrolled in a correspondence course to learn book-keeping and eventually set up in business for herself, working from home when she needed to, and being out and about when she could.

Home work

◆ Do something challenging with your time.

◆ Do a correspondence course or, better still, go to college.

◆ Learn something for the sake of learning, or study for a profession you'd like to do when the kids are old enough or you feel ready.

♦ Don't stand still too long or you'll stagnate.

♦ Have a goal in mind so that you know where you're going.

♦ Get a hobby or do some voluntary work.

♦ Keep fit: exercise encourages your brain to release feel-good chemicals (such as serotonins and endorphins) that ward off depression.

♦ Mix with people you don't know, and think of new ways to stretch yourself. This will help to remind you that you're alive and that you have potential.

The guilt monster

Linda's girls are now in their teens, but looking back over the last decade makes her shudder. 'Working out who to put first, my kids or my job, left me in a constant state of guilt. My boss was great and understood, but that didn't make me feel any better about regularly arriving late, having to leave early, or showing up at the office with a sick child, a blanket and a stack of colouring books. In fact, it made me feel worse.'

Linda found herself in a guilt trap: the more accommodating her boss was, the worse she felt about having to 'let him down', so she worked even harder to make up for it. 'I remember once, my youngest didn't stop vomiting till 2 a.m. At five o'clock I woke her up to ask if she was feeling better – better enough to go to school! It sounds awful, but the thought of phoning my boss to say that I had to take more time off to look after yet another sick child was too much to bear. The kids really did have to put up with a lot.'

Linda was mainly guilty of having expectations much too high for herself. She's a perfectionist and never does anything by halves, so not being able to put 100 per cent into both family and work left her worried that she wasn't doing either job well enough. She spent ten years of her life in a state of guilt, and was even now beating herself up for that.

Mantras for the guilty

Try saying these sentences aloud whenever you feel guilty about work and your kids.

1 I am doing my very best for my family, and my best is all I've got.

2 Expecting more than I can achieve is setting myself up to fail. If I expect reasonable things, I can succeed.

3 My best can't be ten out of ten every day. I'll keep my expectations in line with what's going on in my life.

4 I'm learning alongside my kids, and I'm not afraid to admit when I get it wrong.

5 Beating myself up is pointless and self-destructive. I can be kind to myself even when I feel undeserving because that's when I need kindness most.

6 It's not my job to please everyone.

7 I am proud of being a single parent. It's down to me that we are surviving.

8 My kids will survive this and so will I.

9 It's OK for me to want things for myself.

10 I'm a good role model because I try hard, not because I'm perfect.

Guilt cements us in shame, where we cannot grow or move forward. If we're not careful, it will come to rule our lives, our self-esteem and our parenting styles. That's why we have to banish it from our life. It's a worthless feeling, with absolutely no benefits or resolution. It's merely a big stick we use to punish ourselves. If we want to be happy, even fleetingly, we have to let it go. We need to forgive ourselves for making mistakes, and remind ourselves that tomorrow is a new day when we can do things differently if we're prepared to make the effort to change things.

Your children

1
2
3

Whenever I talk about children's needs, parents start feeling guilty and defensive, afraid of criticism and judgement. The truth is that we are all our own harshest critics and cruellest judges. As single parents, we make things worse by projecting that we won't be able to meet our kids' needs all by ourselves. The truth is that if our kids feel as though we're trying our best, they'll feel loved and valued, and if we get that right even some of the time, then we're already meeting most of their needs right there.

What follows is not included as a stick to beat yourself with. Read it with a view to what you can learn rather than what you can kick yourself for. Accepting that we won't meet all our children's needs all the time, and forgiving ourselves for that in advance will make life easier on us and them.

Get on with life

Kids are deeply affected when their parents split up, no matter how hard we try to protect them. They each express their feelings differently, but however they do so, it's important to let them know it's OK for them to have their own feelings and that they will be different from ours. What they want most is for both parents to be happy again. Feeling guilty about 'putting the kids through it' will slow that process down, dragging your pain out and ultimately theirs too.

The words 'parent' and 'guilt' seem to go hand in hand, and single parents get a double dose. But while you're lashing yourself about the injustices you and your partner have visited upon your kids by splitting up, they're tapping their feet, waiting for you to say it's OK for them to get on with things. I've met parents who just couldn't let their guilt go, and, as a result, ended up trying to raise their kids from the bottom of the Guilt Well, which was not only hard on them, but also miserable for their kids. Guilt has its own special consequences on our parent–child relationship, and none of them are good.

A mum once said to me, 'If I forgive myself, I'll be letting myself off the hook, and why should I get off scot-free when the kids still have to pay for the fact that we couldn't make it work? If we'd stayed with their father, they'd have two parents, a garden to play in and their own rooms. Why wouldn't I feel bad?'

She saw her separation as a blight on her children's lives, and couldn't be persuaded otherwise. She felt that there was a price to pay for her happiness and that the kids had had to pay it. After lots of investigation, this turned out to be a story she was telling herself so she wouldn't have to face the big, bad world and start living again. Being in perpetual guilt about her boys meant she could justify 'giving up' her own life to make it up to them. She thought she was meeting their needs, but she was in fact meeting her own. Meanwhile, they were walking all over her, challenging her in every way they could to make her stand up to them and be the bad-tempered, strong-willed, unyielding mum they'd known and loved all their lives. This new, pushover mum made them feel insecure and leaderless.

It takes a lot of energy to hold on to negative memories and feelings, valuable energy that our kids need us to spend on them – having fun, talking, playing and relaxing with them.

Guilt makes us	Kids need us to
Inconsistent	Be consistent
Needy of approval	Approve of them
Easy to manipulate	Keep firm boundaries
Insecure	Make them feel safe
Miserable	Be happy alongside them

Keep learning

Most of us dreamt of the kind of parents we were going to be while our offspring were still in the womb. We imagined ourselves patient and gentle, understanding and wise, firm and attentive. Few of us imagined ourselves totally losing it with our kids, or feeling so beaten down that we'd end up letting them do what they want, or becoming so shut off from them that we don't know who they are. No one, single or otherwise, can prepare for the demands of being a parent, which is why it's so important that we don't pretend to know it all. Our kids won't be unnerved by our not knowing what to do if they see us trying to find out. They need us to show them that there's no shame in asking for help so that when they in turn need answers, they won't be afraid to ask the questions.

Some of us think that we should 'just know' what to do in every parenting eventuality, but 'growing' children is a free-form experiment that's in a constant state of flux. The more information we have, the better equipped and more confident we'll feel about the job we're doing. The more confident we are, the safer our kids will feel in our hands. So when a new issue arises, do the research: read, watch TV programmes, surf the Net and ask friends and family about their experiences. Saying 'I don't know, but I'm going to find out' is infinitely more valuable to our kids than 'I know it all and my word is law'.

Know what they need

Being able to identify our needs is actually a very sophisticated process that we struggle to master all the way into adulthood. Children need us to do it for them because they can't do it for themselves. They get their needs all mixed up with their wants, and their wants confused with their fears, and their fears muddled with facts, which is why they need us to help work it out for them when they're little, and to give them the space to work it out for themselves later on. When they're babies we learn how to translate their noises, facial expressions and cries into demands for feeding, winding, changing, stimulation and comfort. Then, as they get older, we implement routines to help us guess what's coming up next so that we can be there, ready to meet their needs just as they appear; and when they're teenagers, we try to teach them how to meet their own. It's a tricky job, especially if we're not even sure how to recognise our own needs, but no matter how often we guess wrongly, our hit rate is likely to be a hundred times better than theirs.

Play detective

There's almost no point in asking our kids 'What's wrong?' Whether it's a teenager on a diet who has decided you wouldn't understand, a three-year-old having nightmares who has no vocabulary to describe the horrors, or a pubescent 12-year-old who's still bedwetting and hiding the evidence, our children present us with all sorts of imaginable and unimaginable mysteries to solve. Asking them what's wrong just leaves them feeling either stupid for not knowing the answer, or insecure because if *you* don't know, who does? What they *want* is for us to fix, take responsibility for or ignore their problems. What they *need* is for us to treat their problems like gentle investigations, working with them side by side or from the sidelines. This might mean interviewing other people in their lives and looking at the context of the problem, taking every detail into consideration. It's worth noting here that not all problems can be solved, and sometimes all we can do is to sit with them in their despair, holding their hand and telling them that they won't always feel this way. Look at the following example:

Solving a mystery

Your six-year-old starts to complain of tummy aches last thing at night, kicking up a fuss, and refusing to stay in bed and go to sleep. He gives a repeat performance in the morning, dragging his heels getting dressed and not eating his breakfast.

Possible motives

♦ He doesn't want to be away from you.
♦ He doesn't want to go to school.
♦ He's poorly (unlikely in this instance).
♦ He's naughty and just wants to make your life miserable.

Process of elimination

You're the first witness, so begin by bringing yourself in for questioning. Have there been any changes to your routine at home? Have you been your normal self? (Children are hyper-vigilant when it comes to their parents' moods. They might not understand what's going on, but they know when something's up.) If you're in the clear, move on to the other adults in his life – babysitters, grandparents and so forth. What have they noticed? Talk to the child's other parent about what he knows and whether there have been any changes or events in his life that your child may have been privy to. If you come up blank, move on to the next possibility – school. Maybe the teacher or the dinner ladies will be able to shed some light on the mystery. Is your child sociable? Who does he play with? Has he been behaving differently recently? Even if you never find a probable cause, seeking to understand is an act of love because it bothers to look a bit further than 'He's just plain old naughty', even if that's what your investigation eventually concludes.

'Naughty' is an easy label we put on our kids when we're too tired, angry or busy to look for a real explanation.

Look after yourself so they don't have to

Unless you've been supremely disciplined about keeping your untidy emotions under wraps, the chances are that your kids have seen you rage, snot and blubber in the period leading to the break-up, throughout it and beyond. With the other parent out of the picture, they feel it's their job to rescue us, and we can get so lonely and depressed that occasionally it's welcome and we allow it. While there's nothing wrong with getting a cuddle, we need to be careful not to make the kids our confidantes. They need us to take care of ourselves no matter how fragile and incapable we might feel because once they make themselves responsible for our happiness, our unhappiness becomes their problem too, and then you have to ask who's parenting who?

If we make sure that we get the support we need from family, friends or professional counsellors, staying the parent won't feel so hard to do. Kids need to know that it's OK for them to feel all their feelings without being afraid of upsetting you, and that can be hard, especially in the early days.

It's not easy to comfort a child who's missing his mum or dad while you're still seething with rage about being left, or still beating yourself up for having left, or still in shock after being bereaved. If you hope to stay compassionate and open to hearing them, you're going to have to make sure that someone is doing that for you.

Feel for them

Our kids' emotional lives are every bit as complicated as our own (at least to them). We spend our lives developing coping mechanisms to deal with pain and fear, love and loss, grief and rage, but for children, who have all the feelings and none of the experience, life can be scary and confusing. With no former knowledge that feelings pass or that just because we feel something doesn't mean it's true, emotions can present a real threat to safety. The most natural thing for us to do with unpleasant feelings is to block them out. Most adults learn from bitter experience that hiding from them doesn't make them go away, and that buried feelings can lie in wait for an (in)opportune moment to reveal themselves, perhaps making you burst into tears because you miss the bus, or they can pop up in disguise as something else, such as recurring anger without just cause. This is also true for children whose blocked feelings may turn into violent outbursts, disobedience or hyperactivity. Teenagers might just turn the music up louder to drown out the thoughts and feelings that upset them, or they might develop anxious symptoms, becoming sullen and insular. Our kids need us to be their emotional interpreters, gently encouraging them to face up to whatever it is that's making them unhappy or scared, and helping them to come up with ways of taking control of their situation and feeling a bit more powerful in their own lives.

Translate for them

We naturally do a lot of translating when the children are infants, and only we understand their funny ways of speaking, but we tend to stop once they learn to speak for themselves. We need to remember that just because they know how to talk doesn't mean they have the skills to communicate everything they want to say. While they're getting to grips with a world of new experiences, they need us to continue our work of translating the complexities of life into a language they can understand, and commentating on their world view with an experienced voice.

The following is a 'perfect' example of an adult translating a painful experience for a three-year-old. I wouldn't really expect anyone to pull this off quite as suggested, but it'll give you the idea.

BOY: Mummy, please may I have an ice cream?

MUM: No, it's too close to teatime and you'll spoil your appetite.

BOY: But Mummy, I said please.

MUM: I know you did and that was lovely, but the answer is still no. *(Boy goes into a tantrum, saying Mummy is mean and he doesn't love her. Mum stays completely calm; she knows it's his job to want ice cream as much as it's hers to regulate his diet.)*

MUM: You look like you're feeling really angry.

BOY: *(Screaming at the top of his voice)* I am really angry.

MUM: I'm sorry to hear that. It's horrible feeling angry, isn't it? *(She gives him permission to feel his anger, and lets him know it's both normal and acceptable.)*

BOY: *(Starting to cry but still shouting)* YES, IT IS.

MUM: *(Picking up on the tears, she focuses on the new feeling emerging.)* And now you look really sad.

BOY: *(Responding to the softness in her voice)* I am really sad 'cause I can't have an ice cream. *(Boy is accepting that he can't have what he wants and that it's OK to feel upset about it.)*

MUM: When I'm sad, I like to have a cuddle. Would you like a cuddle? *(Boy nods his head and climbs on to mum's knee for a cuddle.)*

The reality is that when we have to say 'no', children get upset, and we hate it when our kids are upset, so we try appealing to a sense of logic we suddenly find ourselves imagining they have. The thing to remember when attempting to have a logical debate with a three-year-old (or a thirteen-year-old for that matter) is that they cannot argue on our level, so time and again we're surprised to find ourselves reduced to arguing on theirs.

If you manage to rise above the temptation to argue with your kids on their level, you're a better parent than I. They know how to wind us up and wind us in. When my son was young, and before I knew better, I routinely argued with him, and he routinely won because you can't beat a child at childishness, no matter how childish you can be. Better by far to outsmart them using logic, persuasion and distraction.

Remember...

◆ Give them the right to express their feelings, whatever they are.
◆ Name their feelings until they can name their own.
◆ Empathise with them; try to put yourself in their shoes.
◆ Don't take it personally.

Let them have their say

Actively listening to our kids is not an automatic reflex; it's a learnt technique and is therefore an effort. Listening might not sound that challenging, but when there's more than one child doing the talking, and their simultaneous non-stop chatter is ruining *Coronation Street*, the football or just having a minute to yourself, it can feel pretty challenging. Thankfully, they don't need us to be listening attentively all the time, but when they do, we'd better be prepared because if our kids don't feel we're listening when they're really trying to talk to us, they're likely to feel we're not interested in what they have to say. If they feel that too often, they might stop trying to talk to us at all.

Listening

There are two types of listening – active and passive. One is engaged and the other is disengaged. All parents know the latter. Come teatime up and down the country, homes are echoing with parents dutifully putting on their 'how interesting' voices while they actually ignore the chat, chat, chatting of their kids. 'Really? Wow! That's great, darling. Uh huh. Mm. Sorry, what did you say?' Managing to sound as though we're listening without actually doing so is an acquired skill that comes about as a matter of survival, especially if you've got several voices trying to engage you in the wonders of their day. Having a partner would mean that we could cleverly divert the kids' demand for attention on to the other parent while we get on with cooking the tea and mentally processing our own day. Not having one means that your need for mental space and processing time will have to wait.

> ♦♦ *You have the right to express the views you have and for your views to be listened to in anything that affects you* ♦♦
>
> Advice to children, UN Convention on the Rights of the Child (1999)

Children do exactly the same with us, which is why it's no good issuing commands if they're in front of the telly or at the Playstation: they don't hear because they're not really listening. 'Did you hear me?' might get a response, 'Yeah,' but unless you've managed to break their focus from the screen, there's no guarantee that they'll have registered your existence, never mind what you asked.

Active listening is easier to describe if you think of the way you ask them to listen to you when you're trying to tell them something that you really need them to hear. We get them to make eye contact with us, we say the same thing two or three times in different ways, and then we get them to repeat what we've said back to us so we know they've got the message. When we actively listen to them, we help them to feel understood by reflecting back what we hear using different words and asking questions that encourage further investigation.

Let them have a go

Allowing my son to make his own mistakes has been the single most difficult aspect of parenting for me. I'm impatient by nature, and it's not easy for me to stand back and watch someone struggle. Sometimes I'd insist on taking over a task because time was short, but mostly it was my patience that was in short supply. This is one of the complaints my son makes about his childhood that has me cringing in shame: I made him feel incompetent. He likes to tell people the story about how I bought him shoes with Velcro fastening because I wasn't patient enough to teach him to tie shoelaces. That wasn't strictly true; I did teach him, but then he insisted on doing it for himself even when we were in a rush. Velcro was simply my way of getting him to school on time. The other thing I did regularly was to redo jobs he'd already done. It seems I was a bit of a control freak back then (there are those who'd say I still was), and while I might've had things exactly the way I wanted them, all I'd managed to teach him was that if a job wasn't going to be done perfectly, it wasn't worth doing at all. He has since forgiven me as he is now exactly the same!

Support their relationship with the other parent

Easier said than done, right? I envy the ex-couple who are mature enough to put their issues to one side long enough to work out what's best for their kids. I'm not saying that no one manages it – lots of parents do every day – but it can be hard to override the natural compulsion to walk away from your ex and keep walking, just as you would had you not had kids together. In the days before we had children, breaking up was painful, but at least we got to move on without looking back.

A REWARDING ACTIVITY

Love is not something we feel; it's something we do. Love is an activity. The feeling we call love is actually joy, which is the reward received for the act of loving.

Having to engage with someone while you're trying to get over them, or while you're still furious, hurt or guilty, can feel like torture, but we do it (or at least try to) because we know it's the right thing for our kids. The truth is that it's sometimes too much, and the only thing we can do is ask someone else to act as a go-between until we've moved on enough to take over. Whether your partner died, left you, or gave you no choice but to leave, your children still have a right to choose how to feel about both their parents, which means that we need to keep our personal feelings about the absent mum or dad to ourselves where we can. And where we can't, we have to be prepared to apologise and find a way to explain ourselves.

Chill out

No one really knows how much of what we do contributes to the person our child will grow into. It seems that what counts most is that kids have a consistent sense that they are valued by someone. Ultimately, I believe that as long as we can say that we make our kids feel loved most of the time, we're on target to raising happy, secure children, despite the chaos that might reign the rest of the time.

Children aged 0–5

Being the single parent of a child or children under five is unbelievably demanding and would test the patience of a saint. For those of us who are far from saintly, it's just plain old stressful. Their needs are non-stop from the second they wake until they (finally) drop off to sleep. Finding ways to have a shower, make phone calls, clean the house or even go to the loo become a daily challenge once they start crawling, and if you have more than one pre-schooler, you will already know that one pair of hands simply isn't enough. There are loads of other parents in exactly the same boat, and if you do the research, you'll find a wealth of crèches and toddler groups that cost little or nothing. Here you'll get some adult conversation while the children get a lesson in socialising with their peers.

World view

It's impossible to imagine the world from a small child's point of view. Putting ourselves in their shoes would be like trying to imagine not recognising the written letters of our own name, or not knowing that two plus two equals four. We can't unlearn the wisdom and logic that has formed the basis of our understanding of everything, so we cannot regress to a time when we thought as they did. This is why we project 'knowingness' on to our children – because we can't imagine what not knowing looks like. I have heard parents of babies under a year old pronounce them as 'cheeky', 'manipulative' or 'spoilt', when actually it's impossible for that to be the case. Academically speaking, those kinds of behaviour require sophisticated conscious thought structures that can measure action and consequences in a consistent manner so as to form a qualitative outcome. I know we think our two-year-olds are brilliant, but seriously…!

Development in the 0–5s

At first children watch everything all the time. They 'download' more information in the first two years of life than science knows how to measure. Lots of touch, softly spoken words, frequent eye contact and a solid routine will ensure all their needs are met, and while it's tiring because there's no one to share the night-time waking, feeds and so on, it's a breeze compared to the next stage. The drive for independence instinctively encourages them to take their first steps towards the parent–child separation process that will one day mean they can take care of themselves (or so they tell me). Wanting to do things their way and in their own time often conflicts with our need to get somewhere or do something, which is one reason the twos are terrible. Another is the sheer frustration children feel at having an urgent want and not having the verbal skills to put in a request. Even if they do manage to make us understand what they want, they then have to put up with our constant thwarting of their desires while not being able to understand the good reasons we have for saying 'no'. By the time they're three, their newly acquired vocabulary reduces some of their frustration, but increases ours as the little voices we longed to hear ('Can you say "mummy"?') begin to pierce every waking minute. The tantrums thankfully subside, but only to make way for the never-ending stream of unanswerable questions.

> 'Mummy, why are trees green?'
> 'Because of a substance called chlorophyll.'
> 'Mummy.'
> 'Yes?'
> 'What's a substance?'

The good news? School's just around the corner.

The split

The world of the pre-schooler is very small, so everyone and everything in it is very important. When major changes are made to that world, such as a house move, different childcare arrangements or a disappearing parent, a small child is likely to experience them as very unsettling and can become anxious as a result. Some separations instantly alter every aspect of a child's life, but even when just a few changes have taken place, we need to keep our eyes peeled for any emotional consequences they might be suffering. It's not possible to protect them from their feelings, and even if we could, we shouldn't. Recovering from life's ups and downs is how we learn to negotiate life on its own terms, and as long as we support them and let them know it's normal to feel whatever they're feeling, they'll get through it and come out the other side stronger and better prepared for life.

SOS

Kids don't speak their feelings – they enact them. Within every 'behaviour' is an embedded emotional code from them to us. If we don't learn to read their distress signals, they'll just get louder and more extreme until they make themselves received and understood.

Stress is contagious

Kids get stressed by the changes in their lives, causing normal child behaviours to become exaggerated, and children's tolerance of even minor amounts of pressure reduces dramatically. It's important that we try to respond to any new or increased problem behaviours with patience, love and understanding, but if we're really stressed too, that's not going to be easy. Instead of struggling alone, make sure everyone else who cares for your child is aware of that extra stress, and that everyone who cares for you knows that you're feeling it too.

Keep an eye open for the following common stress responses in the under-fives:

♦ Disturbed sleep (waking, resisting, early rising)
♦ Night terrors (waking up frightened)
♦ Meanness to a sibling or other children
♦ Sulkiness and refusals
♦ Constant whining or crying
♦ Clinginess

TIPS FOR DEALING WITH A STRESSED CHILD

♦ **Tell** the nursery or nanny what is happening at home so that they can monitor your child's behaviour and notify you of any changes.

♦ **Include** family and friends (and your ex) in your concerns as they might be able to share their experience and help you come up with ideas. At the very least, talking will help get it off your chest.

♦ **Respond** to worsening tantrums with reassurance and kindness because the worse the behaviour, the more upset your child is feeling.

♦ **Plan** things to look forward to. Your child's world has been rocked and the future might not seem so secure any more. Making plans and carrying them out will help restore her sense of security.

♦ **Establish** the new routine as soon as possible and commit to it. Routines make a child's world feel predictable and safe.

♦ **Bend** the rules a little if necessary. As long as you point out the 'special circumstances', you won't undermine the rules themselves.

Discipline and the 0–5s

We shouldn't even be considering discipline where the under-threes are concerned. Our role is to teach, because everything they do is an exercise in basic life learning, and what they need from us is to be nudged and cajoled in the right direction. Ninety-nine per cent of the time when we feel like punishing, telling off or disciplining a small child, we're under stress to some degree: the punishment is a release of tension for our benefit, not theirs. Next time you feel like shouting at your three-year-old or smacking your four-year-old ask yourself how you're feeling and if you were in a better mood or less tired, would you still respond to their behaviour in the same way? Shouting into a pillow and thumping the mattress works just as well in my experience, and doesn't leave a guilty stain on your conscience.

That's not to say we don't have to maintain clear boundaries and start to introduce rules and codes of conduct, such as good manners, proper eating habits and consistent bedtimes. Acceptable and unacceptable behaviours are both taught and learnt. How well your child learns will depend on your teaching.

Positive parenting techniques

Small children respond best to positive phrasing and direction (actually, we all do). Our body language, facial expressions and general approach usually match our intention, so if we tell children angrily to stop doing something we're unhappy with, we're likely to do so in a way that frightens them. While frightening children into behaving better might actually work in the short term, scaring our kids into submission isn't really anybody's notion of ideal parenting. Luckily, there are other ways of getting good behaviour out of our kids, and while it might require a bit more effort than growling at them, it's much more rewarding and doesn't do anything to damage their esteem, their trust or your conscience.

Reward the good and ignore the bad

We often make the mistake of giving bad behaviour much more attention than good. When the kids are quiet and well behaved, it's tempting to use the opportunity to make a phone call or catch up on your emails. Thus we ignore them until they get bored and start playing up, at which point they get the attention they're after. See what we've taught them here? You can avoid this by noticing when they're well behaved and commenting frequently with lots of positive praise and affection. Make sure you describe the behaviour that you're pleased with so they understand exactly what they're doing right. For example: 'I'm really enjoying you sitting quietly and drawing. Shall we stick the picture up somewhere together when you're finished?'

Children of four and five respond well to sticker charts and treats for good behaviour. Rewards don't have to be expensive or extra special – in fact, it's better if they're not. A sticker, a second bedtime story or feeding the ducks in the park are all perfectly appropriate rewards.

Describe the deed, not the doer

Get into the habit of describing the action rather than labelling the child. For example, 'You're a very silly boy' becomes 'That was a very silly thing to do'. Language is hypnotic. Children are looking to us to teach them who they are, and our opinion counts for everything. If we tell them they are silly, naughty, bad or mean, they'll believe us and it will form part of their self-concept. Avoid what sound like positive labels too. Calling a child 'good' because they've been quiet could discourage them from being noisy and restrict their development.

Don't sweat the small stuff

Learn to let some things go. We can't expect children to learn everything all at once. Choosing one or two things to concentrate on at a time will give them more of a chance of getting it right, and won't be so exhausting for you. As human beings can absorb only so much information at any one time, the brain has an automatic filter system that means we take in only a fraction of what is going on around us. Similarly, children take in only a fraction of what you say, so if you want them to hear what matters, say less.

Own the problem

You hate having a messy living room, but your kids won't put their toys away: whose problem is it? You dress your daughter in a Victorian lace dress that cost a fortune and she spills juice all over it: whose problem is it? You're late for work because your son refused to let you dress him: whose problem is it?

Kids press our buttons, and it's tempting to blame them for the ways in which their childish behaviours impact on us, but we mustn't give in. They have no choice but to behave like children; it's not their fault. Replace 'You've made me really angry/upset/late' with 'I feel really cross about the mess/dress/being late'. This way they know it's your feeling and that it's a part of a consequence rather than something they did to you.

Deal with tantrums and other grumpiness

A tantrum is an expression of frustration. The child is not trying to engage us in battle. Those kicking, screaming public paddies might feel personal, but they're not. When a two-year-old hurls herself on the supermarket floor and yells at the top of her voice, she's merely expressing her feelings by the only means available to her and not trying to ruin your day. You won't be making a rod for your own back by letting children have their way occasionally when it won't harm them. We need to use our wisdom and experience to calm, comfort or ignore the child instead of reacting in kind and adding fuel to the fire. The under-threes are behaving instinctively most of the time, and they don't have the intellectual capability to manipulate or get one over on you no matter how hard that is to believe at times. Similarly, the over-threes have no desire to battle you: they just don't understand why you're saying 'no' to them.

Tantrum triggers

The word 'no' is to blame for the majority of tantrums. Other ways of saying 'no' are 'don't', 'stop it' and 'can't'. Kids of any age hate to have their desires thwarted, but it's much worse when they have no means of understanding the reasoning behind it. Telling a four-year-old that he can't have a chocolate bar because he won't be able to eat his tea is pointless. What does he care if he can't eat his broccoli later when the option is chocolate now? It's best to avoid using 'no' words as much as possible. Replace them with 'yes' words instead. For example:

> 'Can I have some chocolate, Mummy?'
> 'Yes, darling, as soon as you've eaten your broccoli.'

Remember the following points if you want to have a quiet life:
Avoid saying 'no' unless you really mean it. It's a hard word to hear and it's full of disappointment and sadness for children. If you really mean 'no', try to come up with an alternative activity or treat that they can have instead.
Save 'no' for dangerous or serious events. These are things that need a strong negative emphasis, such as not going near the oven or not letting go of your hand while crossing the road.

Make 'no' mean 'no'. If you do say it, stick to your word or what they will learn about your 'no' is that it simply means 'pester harder and I shall receive'.

Another good way of avoiding tantrums is to use distraction. Offering logic by way of explanation only moves you closer to that tantrum, but distraction allows you to change the subject rather than engage in a conversation about it.

'But why can't I have it now?'

'I know, why don't we think of things you could do to make the time go faster? How about running around the garden ten times/drawing a picture/watching a cartoon?'

Children are easy to distract at this age. Take advantage of it for, sadly, it will not last!

Case: Sean and Carl

Sean had a really difficult couple of months when his son Carl, aged three and a half, started nursery full time. 'Every day the walk home was a furious battle. He'd be fine until we got to the newsagents, then, like clockwork, he'd ask for sweets and I'd say, "No, we're going home for our tea". He'd then cry, scowl, scream and stamp all the way home. I'd never seen him so naughty before. I assumed he was just picking up bad habits from the other kids, but when I mentioned it to my mum, she laughed and asked if I'd tried taking a banana. It was so obvious, I could've kicked myself: he wasn't naughty – he was hungry.'

All the clues were there, but Sean didn't look. He made the easy mistake of writing the behaviour off as naughtiness. 'Now I take a drink and a light snack for him to eat on the way home. He still asks for sweets, but when I say 'no' he barely blinks. I can't believe I put us both through all that misery for nothing.'

TIPS TO AVOID TANTRUMS

♦ Stick to a regular meal and nap routine. Most tantrums are born of tiredness or hunger, so regularity in eating and sleeping can avoid this.

♦ Don't pick unnecessary fights. Does it really matter if they wear their Spiderman outfit to the supermarket?

♦ Let them do things for themselves or meet them halfway: 'I'll let you tie one shoelace if I can tie the other.'

♦ Remember, you're cleverer than they are. Find creative ways to get them to do what you want without them noticing.

♦ Exercise avoidance tactics: don't battle with them just for the sake of going head to head. If they always kick off at the shops, take distraction materials, or come up with a game to play with them while you shop.

♦ Give specific instructions. Small children take everything literally, so saying 'Tidy up your toys' will overwhelm them. Narrow the task and give a fun incentive, such as: 'How fast do you think you can put all your bricks back in the box?'

Say goodbye to the 'naughty step'

The naughty step has been popularised by recent television programmes about parenting, and has fast become the accepted replacement for smacking or shutting children in their rooms. The theory is sound: a misbehaving child is forced to sit on a designated 'naughty' step or stair and is left alone for a period of time (one minute for every year of her life) in which she is to reflect upon her naughty actions. After the time's up, she has a chance to behave better or repeat the process. My worry is that the 'naughty step' might well get results, but at what cost? Do we really want to use humiliation tactics to teach our children to do as they're told?

'Naughty' is a negative label we tend to use a lot with little ones. As with all labels, it's a judgement, and in this case it is meant to shame a child into behaving differently, which I believe

❞ Letting them get their own way some of the time at this age won't turn them into spoilt brats – it will simply make them easier to manage, and that's a desirable outcome. ❞

can be very damaging to a child's self-esteem. Shame is the feeling we get when we believe that we're bad people and, as such, do not deserve to be loved. It might sound a little dramatic, but it's from the small seeds sown in childhood that huge and complicated adult belief systems are grown.

Using the 'n' word is a hard habit to break, though not impossible. If you're in the habit of calling your child 'naughty', catch yourself and explain that what you meant was that the thing she did was naughty, and then explain why it's naughty and what you would like her to do differently next time. Tell her not to worry – you're there to help her and that you will remind her if she gets it wrong again. This way, she feels as though you're holding her hand through difficult learning terrain and that stumbling is a natural part of the process rather than something to feel ashamed of.

The other problem with the naughty step is that it forces a time out on a pre-schooler who needs our help to process what's happened. Being left alone to 'think about it' is frightening and confusing, and she's unlikely to calm down under such punishing conditions.

Say hello to the 'calm place'

The name of the place where you force your child to take a time out sends a clear message about what you expect to

ATTENTION!

- There is no reward this age group prizes more highly.
- Anything that stands in the way of them getting it is an enemy.
- There's no such thing as bad attention. They'd rather have your smiling eyes upon them, but they'll make do with your angry ones.

happen there. You might, for example, have a 'calm step' or a 'calm chair'. One parent I worked with came up with a brilliant idea, the 'calm square', which was simply a tea towel she took with her everywhere so that when her child behaved in an unacceptable way, she'd whip it out and make him sit on it until he calmed down enough to hear from her why his behaviour wasn't OK.

Time outs arise from the situation, not from you, and are a learning process rather than a punishment, so we need to be there too. Using a calm voice coupled with a kind but firm intention lets children know that as soon as they are calm, you'll talk to them, but until then, you won't. Sit turned slightly away from them and don't make eye contact. If they get off the chair, step or square, put them back and repeat your instruction in the same tone of voice: 'As soon as you're calm, we can talk and have a cuddle.' This is about as powerful a message as any punishment, but with a lot less potential for doing long-term damage to a child's self-esteem.

The three Cs

Trying to be each of the three Cs outlined below will help keep you sane and your child safe.

Calm: Easier said than done, I know, but it takes only two minutes to take some slow, deep breaths and to lower your heart rate enough to allow you to think clearly. Speaking to children in a low, calm tone will get their attention and mean that they actually listen to what you say rather than how you're saying it. Shouting your message in anger or disapproval will just close them down and the lesson will be lost.

Clear: State clearly what your child did wrong, why it was wrong and what the consequences could or will be. The consequences should be appropriate to the crime and age. So if little Jemima has not switched off the TV, despite having been asked several times, an appropriate consequence might be that she isn't allowed to watch TV the following day, rather than an unrelated consequence such as going to her room or having no pudding.

Clever: Hindsight is fantastic, but it's a fat lot of good when you've got a screaming three-year-old who refuses to leave the park. Actually, forethought – seeing things coming – is better. We know where the trouble spots are and when our kids are likely to play up. Be prepared. Don't go anywhere without a snack, paper and crayons, a small treat (bribe), a favourite toy and a fistful of distractions.

Difficult questions

Very young children adapt quickly to change as long as their needs are being met, but there will still be questions – lots of them – and perfectly reasonable ones from their perspective, but potentially painful for us to answer. The other thing is that they ask their questions as and when they think of them and not necessarily when we're in the right mental space to answer thoughtfully and carefully. Obviously, we take deep breaths and do our best to offer the endless reassurances that they need, but let's not be too hard on ourselves about the times we lose it and show a little seething resentment about the ex in front of them. We're only human. Few of us feel like being nice about an ex after breaking up: we've been hurt, disappointed and heartbroken, so having to keep photos of them around our home or listen to the kids chatter on about them can be akin to torture. Put aside five minutes each evening to have a little chat with your children about their day, their feelings and their thoughts to give them a chance to ask their questions when you're best able to answer them the way you want to.

Why doesn't Daddy live with us any more?

'Because he's a two-timing, lying slimeball' might be the truthful answer, but clearly not what little Johnny wants to hear about his hero dad. An extremely reduced and simplified version of the truth is the best strategy. 'Because Daddy and I were having too many arguments and it was making us angry all the time, so we thought it was best.' For every question children ask, ask one in return: 'How do you feel about that?' There's no way of knowing how they're interpreting the information we give them. Open questions like this will help you to know what they've heard and understood by your answers.

All they really need to know (over and over again) is that they are loved in just the same way as they've always been (by both of you), that it wasn't their fault that you split up, and that everything is going to be just fine.

In with the new

Lena doesn't remember introducing her new partner Damien to her four-year-old daughter Shelly, but she does remember the fallout.

Shelly was horrible to Damien for about three years. She refused to have anything to do with him. She wouldn't go to bed if he was there, or eat at the same table. She made up stories about how mean he was to her when I wasn't looking, and while she was transparent most of the time, there were moments when I found myself questioning my judgement. Damien was so patient and gentle with her, but nothing he did changed her mind about him. In the end, I really lost my patience. I'd been through such a horrible time with her dad – didn't I deserve anything for myself?

What Shelly, now 12, had to say, made sense of everything.

I thought Damien wanted to take my mum away. I used to sit on the top stair listening to them in case he was telling lies about me. I thought he was trying to make Mum get rid of me so he could have her to himself. After Dad left we didn't see him for ages, so it was like he didn't exist any more and Mum was all I had left. Damien and me are mates now, but I still get jealous if Mum gives him more attention than me.

As children, it's the things we can take for granted that make us feel secure – that Mummy and Daddy love us no matter what, that we'll be fed when we're hungry, cuddled when we cry and told off when we misbehave. When a parent walks out they undermine one of their children's foundation beliefs – that they won't be abandoned by their parents. For Shelly, her formerly predictable universe had been plunged into random chaos, where parents can literally disappear without warning. If Daddy could leave her, what was to stop Mummy doing the same? Shelly's behaviour was appropriate to the threat as she perceived it. In her confusion and disappointment, Lena unknowingly responded in ways that made things worse. Specifically, she paid lots of attention to Shelly's bad behaviour, not realising that in doing so, she was reinforcing it ('When I'm mean to Damien, Mummy stops focusing on him and concentrates all her attention on me) and getting angry with her daughter probably made Shelly feel her mum was 'on Damien's side' and that his evil plan was in fact working. Losing the battle for Mum's love wasn't an option, so she just tried harder to keep her attention, using the only means available to her.

Had Lena understood the world of fear and mistrust that her daughter was trying to negotiate, she would have been able to reassure her that Damien had no plans to abduct her away from her daughter, help Shelly to understand her own complicated feelings, and pay lots of attention to her better behaviour. Had she done these things, my guess is that the bad behaviour wouldn't have become the three-year emotional storm that it did.

Are you my new daddy?

Cold-shouldering isn't the only unnerving response your pre-schooler could have to your new love interest. They could also attach instantly, projecting all their feelings about their absent parent on to your undoubtedly unprepared new boyfriend or girlfriend. I remember my three-year-old son asking a boyfriend I'd had for about two months if he was his new daddy. I've never seen anyone struck so dumb or scared.

Some kids recede sulkily or become hopelessly shy with new people in their home, which is pretty uncomfortable for all involved. Whatever their response, we can be sure that if we focus on it (negatively or positively), or ignore it, it'll get worse. We need to talk to them about it in a way that acknowledges the problem without negatively or positively reinforcing it, while also managing not to put labels on the behaviour or the child. However, talking to a four-year-old about interpersonal relationships is as tough as it sounds. The following tips should help.

Talking to four- and five-year-olds

If your child's verbal comprehension is up to it, try the four-part message exercise below, but first prepare the ground:

◆ Choose a calm moment when you can focus all your attention on him.

◆ Make it just the two of you or he might get embarrassed.

◆ Get down to his level – it's less threatening and easier to make eye contact.

◆ Make sure there isn't anything going on that's likely to distract him, such as a TV or a radio programme.

◆ Keep your voice and facial expression serious but light.

Four-part 'I' message

This exercise follows exactly the same principles as the earlier one for adults (see page 43), but has been simplified for children.

Part 1: 'I've got a problem that I was hoping you might help me with. Will you help me?'** (Asking for his help makes him a part of the solution and not the problem.)

Part 2: 'When you behave towards my new friend like you did when you [describe most recent event] …'** (Be specific and avoid judging words, such as 'mean', 'bad' and 'selfish'.)

Part 3: '…it makes me feel very sad and upset.'** (Choose just two feeling words. Keep it simple.)

Part 4: 'How can I help you to behave better

next time? (Encourage him by coming up with suggestions – some silly, some serious – and ask his opinion.)

If you don't feel as though he's engaging or he's disengaged, leave it and try again another day. Trying to force a four-year-old to stay focused on a subject of your choosing is completely pointless. At this age, just letting him know seriously and clearly that you don't like something that he is doing and that you want to help him to do it differently is often all that's needed.

Let's be friends

Being introduced to your kids won't be easy for your lover either. They know how important your kids are to you and that you'll be watching how it goes like a hawk. It must be incredibly unnerving, especially if the person in question hasn't much experience of children. Here are a few things you might like to mention before the introduction takes place.

♦ Small children don't observe normal rules of social conduct, so don't expect politeness – in fact, don't expect anything.

♦ If you've got a big nose or you 'smell funny', not only will children tell you, but the expression on their face will show you exactly how they feel about it.

♦ Your approval rating can rise or fall without notice at any time, and you may find yourself being 'punished' for stepping over a line you didn't notice (because it wasn't there yesterday).

♦ Kids stare – a lot.

♦ Kids ask lots and lots of questions. You don't have to answer them all.

♦ If they don't like you, you will know, but it's not a final conclusion. They change their minds – often.

♦ Ignore strange behaviour and reward friendliness with attention.

♦ Don't take it personally.

Love me love my kids

The best we should expect from a new partner is that they will be patient and realise that this is new for everyone involved. We hope that they will develop a relationship of their own with our kids – a bond with clear boundaries and mutual like and respect. Demanding that someone love our kids is unrealistic. Being a step-parent is a whole world away from being your partner, and it's not a simple decision to make, nor is it one that can be made overnight or under pressure. Let things take their course. If they're going to fall in love with your kids or your kids are going to love them back, it won't be because you said they had to or else!

Children aged 6–11

When we refer to 'our childhood' most of us think back to the five short years between six and 11. A certain degree of independence and almost no responsibility make it a time of free play and adventure. Kids of this age can be such enigmas. One minute they've got us raising our eyebrows as pearls of wisdom roll out of their inexperienced mouths, and the next they could be rolling on the floor having a full-blown tantrum. It can be hard to judge what they're capable of understanding, so we underestimate them as often as we overestimate.

It's during these years that our children become less ours and more their own as their personalities and looks say more about who they are than whose genes they inherited. They're no longer mini-versions of us – they're full-colour versions of themselves, with their own ideas to bring to the party. They develop a private life where they have thoughts, events and dreams they don't necessarily want to share with us, and we're no longer their sole source of information as they begin to get their questions answered by friends, television and the Internet. They start to compare their life with the life of others, and learn to feel outraged by the injustices. They learn that they have control over their own future as every adult they meet asks them, 'What are you going to be when you grow up?' The possibilities seem endless. In fact, it's probably the last time in our life where our unlimited imaginations allow us to believe that we can do and be anything we want, and for the next few years at least no one will say otherwise.

On the flipside, children begin to argue with our every suggestion and command. They make excuses and nag us into submission for things they want, turning pester power into an art form. They become cheeky, wilful, rude and stubborn, and most will have a go at telling a lie, cheating, stealing and manipulating in order to get something they want or to get out of trouble. Their friends' opinions have more sway than ours, and almost everyone knows better than we do. They copy our worst behaviour and play it back to us, giving us no right to admonish them for it because their innate sense of fair play will have them reminding us that we did it first. They learn where all our buttons are and they play them like piano keys, sending us up and down the extremes of our own emotional scales. They'll also learn during these years what it is to disappoint us and make us cry, lose our temper and frighten us, which will in turn frighten them as they wake up to the unnerving realisation that their parents are fallible, vulnerable and human.

I don't know about anyone else, but I really didn't sign up for any of that. I signed up for a fat bouncing baby who'd adore me and simply want to be adored back. There were times I looked at my eight-, nine-, ten-year-old son – all arms, legs and his ever-smart lip – and wondered if my statutory rights had been affected.

World view

Imagining what the world looks like from the point of view of a primary school child is tricky for at least two reasons. First, we can't imagine what it's like not to know what we know now (see the 0–5 world view, page 102), and second, as our brain remembers a lot of detail about this time in our own history, we tend to project our own experience on to our children – as a result, we're not seeing the world from their perspective at all, but from a distant memory of our own perspective. I say this to encourage and remind us not to make assumptions about our kids' experience of their life. If we want to understand them, we have to really listen to what they're trying to say, and judge them as separate individuals in a different time, in different circumstances and with a different personality than our child-hood self. Just because we've been eight doesn't mean we know what it is for our kids to be eight. If we want to know, we have to ask them.

Development of 6–11s

Children go through so many different stages during this time that it's hard to keep track. Sometimes the shift happens over-night – literally. My son had always been incredibly affection-ate, so it took me completely by surprise when kisses and cud-dles at the school gates were abruptly abolished by him one morning without warning, quickly followed by hand-holding in the street, mouth/face wiping, clothing/hair adjustments, and any public displays of affection or, indeed, any action that could be described as 'motherly'. He was around seven, and I remember feeling real sadness that my little boy's baby years were well and truly over.

If one statement could sum up this time, it would be 'It's not fair'. Children are constantly balancing the books. They mark down every time you give their sibling more chips, or when you short-change them on their bedtime story, or when you don't meet your promises. At least we don't have to worry too much about their needs not being met because by hook or by crook they'll make sure they are, even if that means nagging us to death. If we don't step up our game to meet their newly refined manipulative skills, they'll blindly and without conscience walk all over us. Thankfully, as long as we mean to be fair, we can appeal to their sharp sense of justice to get our needs met too. It's never too early to bring in the concept of you scratch my back and I'll scratch yours.

False accounting

Splitting up, no matter what the circumstances, is draining; it leaves us feeling confused, bruised, furious, grief-stricken and, in some cases, shocked and traumatised. Trying to survive all that and still go to work, maintain a home and look after the kids all by ourselves means budgeting our energy. Like any budget, it means we have to shave our outgoings, and when the resource we're trying to spread further is our energy, attending to the kids' daily emotional needs can be the first thing to go. In a list of priorities that includes 1.) Work or lose house, 2.) Hold on to sanity by a fine thread, and 3.) Find a reason to keep going, it's easy to see how that happens. However, it's false accounting because all those unmet needs of theirs are actually quietly building up to an explosive crescendo of especially bad behaviour.

Children want to be independent, but they want to do it under our watchful, approving eyes so that we can both validate their experiences and keep them safe. If they feel as though we take our eyes off them for too long, they'll do whatever's necessary to bring our attention back to them, even if it means them having to risk our disapproval as a result. If we remember that our approval is the most valued parenting prize of all, the fact that they're willing to give it up just to get our attention should tell us how important it is to them that they remain in focus. This might go some of the way to explaining why our kids seem to really pick their moment when it comes to misbehaving.

The effects of stress

When children experience a major change in their life, such as a parent leaving or a house move, all the predictable elements of their life become temporarily unstable, and for a while at least this level of insecurity is likely to lead to stressful feelings.

The behaviours listed below are all normal in children of primary school age, but a marked increase in any one or combination of them for a sustained period of time could mean that a child is suffering some stress. In this case, it might be more prudent to respond directly to the source rather than try to tackle the behaviour.

Normal behaviour in 6–11s
◆ Irritability
◆ Whinging
◆ Clinginess

♦ Questioning authority
♦ Challenging boundaries
♦ Avoiding school
♦ Nightmares (fear of the dark)
♦ Withdrawal from peers
♦ Loss of interest in school

When they were little we could bank on the fact that general grumpiness was usually down to a basic need not being met, such as the need for sustenance or attention. Now they're older and more complicated we might have to look a little further for answers. But before we can do anything to help, we have to be able to identify what's wrong. Use the following acronym to dismiss the most likely culprits first.

HALT – ask yourself are your children feeling:
H – hungry? **A** – angry? **L** – lonely? **T** – tired?

Any one of these feelings can distort our emotions and make them seem insurmountable. If we're hungry, no amount of talking, comforting or shouting is going to get rid of the pangs, and if we're tired, things are only going to get worse until we've rested. In this age group, loneliness and anger can often be resolved with a little extra one-on-one time, a cuddle and a chat. If you think your children might be stressed, exercise a bit more patience with their behaviours, but don't ignore them. They still need to understand that negative behaviours have negative consequences though the consequence you choose should reflect a lesson in taking responsibility for their feelings rather than taking them out on everyone else. Look at the following example.

Event: Your child hits his younger sibling, making him cry – yet again.

A loving response: Tell him firmly but calmly that you want to speak to him alone. Let him know that under *no circumstances* is it OK for him to hit his brother (use a stern facial expression and tone of voice). Explain that hitting is the action of a bully, and as you know he's not really a bully, you'd like to find out why he's acting like one.

Help him take an emotional inventory, bearing in mind that he might not want to tell you the exact nature of the problem. Ask leading questions designed to help him find his own answers.

'You don't have to tell me everything, but it'll help me understand if you can say what you're feeling inside.'

'You seem to be angry or worried about something. Do you know what it is?'

'Is it your brother's fault?'

'When you hit your brother, does it make the angry feeling go away?'

'I understand that your feelings are hard to cope with, but hitting your brother isn't the right way to deal with them. Do you agree?'

'How do you imagine your brother feels when you hit him? 'Do you think apologising to your brother is the right thing for you to do now?'

'It takes a lot of courage to be honest and talk about feelings. I hope that next time you want to hit out, you'll come and talk to me about how you're feeling instead. Well done!'

Then pat yourself on the back too because it takes a lot of effort not to react to your instinctive desire for retribution, and punish, shout or threaten. This way our kids might actually learn something that makes a difference.

Lying, stealing, cheating and other coping mechanisms

Kids lie to get themselves out of trouble or into favour. They steal because they want something they know you won't allow them to have, and they cheat because winning feels better than losing. It's all a normal part of the growing process, but as parents, we can feel so frightened by these particular behaviours in our kids that we try to shame them out of doing it again before it 'gets out of control'. None of these behaviours indicate that our kids are budding criminals or unlovable losers. It simply means that they've discovered new ways of getting what they want, and until we teach them otherwise, they'll continue to do it.

We've all lied. Most of us still do when we feel a situation warrants it. Sometimes we catch children out, and sometimes they get away with it. All we can do is let them know how their lies make us feel, and point out the consequences (lack of trust – the boy who cried wolf, and suchlike). Help them to work out why they lied. Were they afraid of something? The same goes for stealing, except they should be made to return the item and apologise to the person they stole from. With cheating, explain that winning

> ♦♦ *Never use the police as a threat. One day your children's safety might depend on their being able to approach one.* ♦♦

feels good because of the achievement, therefore cheating drains all the good feeling from winning. Remember to praise any action they take to repair the damage because in the end, the behaviour that's rewarded with the most attention will be the one repeated in the future.

INTERNAL AFFAIRS

Make a special family postbox out of an empty tissue box and put it somewhere out of view with some paper and pens nearby. Explain to the kids that it's for internal family mail; that it's a great way to tell someone something that you might find hard to say to their face. Anyone can write a note to another member of the family and post it (include stamps and sealable envelopes for letters to the absent parent if it feels appropriate), and anyone can check the postbox at any time of day to see if there's any mail for them, but they must not open other people's letters. Play the game. Write letters telling them how proud or happy you are with their correct behaviour – it will encourage more of it in the future. Open the postbox up to grandparents too.

Shame on you

Shame is the most destructive force we ever use against our children. We shame them to hurt them because we believe that pain is the only real motivation for learning, but if that were true, we'd still be caning our kids in school and it wouldn't be illegal for parents to hit them. Shaming is worse than smacking because the internal handprint of a shaming remark might never fade, affecting the way that children see themselves for the rest of their life. How many of us were told by a teacher that we were 'stupid' or 'lazy'? These are tough labels to shake. There is never a good reason to make children feel bad about the person they are when it's just as effective to make them feel bad about what they've done and not injure their vulnerable ego.

The power of labels

Children learn who they are from us. If we tell them they're stupid, lazy, selfish or mean, they'll believe us: it will become a part of their self-concept. What's more, if we do it with a tone of voice and a facial expression that suggests these characteristics are unacceptable or unlovable, we're implying that they're bad people because of it. Most of the labels we stick on children in anger or impatience are actually for everyday normal human behaviour. Who isn't sometimes lazy or selfish? Telling children that being selfish makes them unlovable will leave them with a constant nagging feeling that to take care of their own needs ahead of others' makes them bad people. My therapy practice is full of people who grew up failing because of exactly this kind of self-defeating myth.

What's the answer? Avoid all accusatory words: their only purpose is to punish. Look for positive ways to describe the behaviour you want your children to engage in more rather than focus on the one you want less of. For example, 'You'll feel so pleased with yourself after you've finished your homework', not 'Only lazy boys don't do their homework'.

Discipline and the 6–11s

The desire to punish is not discipline, it's retribution, and it's scarily easy to feel when there isn't another adult to take over when you're at your wits' end. 'He's a selfish little brat,' you might yell about your son after a long, hard day, to which a partner might reply, 'No, he's not. He's just a kid who doesn't get the rules yet.' Without that balancing perspective, it can be hard to keep your head. As single parents, it's essential we take a time out between Reaction and Action because there's no one else there to protect our kids from us at our most irrational.

Replace the word 'punishment' with 'consequence'. Making sure that your children realise their actions have consequences is a vital part of life learning, but that's not the same as punishing them. Punishing them is about getting your own back for their upsetting you. It's the 'he-hit-me-so-I-hit-him-back' mentality that occurs between children who don't have any concept of conflict resolution. It's very tempting to shrink down to their level sometimes, but when we feel like 'hitting them back', it's time to step away from the temptation, take a deep breath and grow back up.

Replace the word 'discipline' with 'teach' – it's a great reminder that our job is to teach our kids, not judge them. When we're teaching we don't say that our child is selfish and mean because of his actions, we explain that his actions have had negative consequences that he needs to consider if he's to make better decisions next time.

To be disciplined, we must be calm, collected and fully in control of our own responses. If we're not in control, we're out of control, and therefore in no state to discipline the undisciplined as we are one of them.

The three Cs

Trying to be each of the three Cs outlined below will help to keep you sane and your child safe.

Calm: Stress is contagious due to a human messaging system designed to alert each other to potential danger. If we lose control of ourself and start ranting and raving, we're more likely to scare our kids than teach them anything. When we feel scared, we lock down into fight or flight mode, which for children means either arguing back or receding into themselves until the threat is over. No one wants to scare their kids, but can we really know just how terrifying we are when we're enraged? Taking deep breaths over two minutes gives us a chance to collect our thoughts and remember that we're the adults and therefore the example.

Clear: Talk through your feelings about your children's actions with another adult before confronting them about it. Sometimes it's hard to know how much of our anger, disappointment, hurt or concern is about them and how much of it is about the stressful load we're carrying in our life generally. Work, relationships, loneliness, the entire burden of responsibility for our family take their toll every day. We need to be clear about what's what so that we don't end up using our kids as an emotional dumping ground.

Clever: Use the techniques outlined earlier and below. Be one step ahead of them. We have infinitely more wisdom and experience than children do, yet we often abandon all that knowledge in favour of a childish instinctive response that we end up feeling guilty for later. If you don't have the next step right there and then, don't be afraid to announce that you haven't got the answer yet and that you'll get back to them. Be the adult. If you can't, take some time out till you can.

Disciplinary techniques for 6–11s

Here are some ways of keeping children in line without damaging their unstable ego (sense of self).

1 Three strikes and out

This method works only if it's used consistently. The threat, which needs to be appropriate to the misdemeanour, must always be carried out every time, so be careful what you threaten. Look at this example:

First strike: 'I've asked you to lay the table and you've ignored me. This is your first strike. Please lay the table.'

Second strike: 'This is now your second strike. If you haven't laid the table by... [state the time, or point to where the big hand on the clock will be, or count to 30], you will not be allowed any pudding.' (Then ask the child to repeat what you've just said back to you.) 'Tell me what I've just said so that I know you've heard and understood.'

Third strike: 'This is your third strike. You have not done what I asked, despite my warnings, so now I will lay the table and you will not get any pudding, as agreed.'

Whether there are tears and tantrums come pudding time, or if they beg to lay the table there and then, stay calm and say it's too late: you offered them a choice and they chose. Next time they should act on the second or even first warning.

2 Time out

The purpose of a time out is to teach that sometimes it's better to remove yourself from a situation than to let it play out – where there is aggression, for example. Sometimes we send children on a time out because *we* need to calm down too. Stick to the rule of giving them one minute for every year of their life, and make sure they understand exactly why they've been given the time out in the first place.

Time outs work best if the children are not sent to their room. Being shut up in a room with a TV, DVD, PS2 and numerous other distractions will not encourage them to ponder their misbehaviour. It's best to make them sit somewhere they can still hear family activities, but not close enough to take part in them. When we remove children from a situation involving others, we deprive them of attention and a chance to be where the action is. Also, time outs are more effective if they're saved for the big stuff. If we use them for everything, there's a danger we'll dilute their power.

♦♦ *Give yourself a time out if you lose your temper – teach by example.* ♦♦

Introducing a new set-up

There's no pulling the wool over the eyes of 6–11s – they're far too canny, so if you've got a new love interest, it's best to be upfront about it or hide it properly. If you've lied about the nature of your relationship and your new 'friend' is discovered naked in your bed, your kids will feel betrayed. If you have a reason to keep your relationship secret, then keep it secret. Don't take risks with your child's trust.

It's not ideal to introduce anyone in the first few months after the other parent has left the house. If possible, give your kids time to get used to the first change before introducing a new one, even if you left your partner because you met someone else. That someone else will have absolutely no chance of gaining your kids' like or respect if they end up carrying the can for the break-up.

Obviously, you'll want to spend time alone with your new lover, but don't expect your kids to be pleased about it. They liked it better when they had you all to themselves. If you pay less attention to them when your new lover is around, your children will have no choice but to compete, and that means trouble. Make sure they know that they're still the main love of your life: keep them in focus in front of your guest so that everyone knows who's at the top of your list.

The children are not obliged to like your new partner, and it won't help your cause if they get the impression you're not going to give them a choice. Let them come forward in their own time and in their own way. Your new partner is an adult, and while it will be tricky for them too, it's the kids who need your special attention, so make sure you remember whose feelings need protecting.

Your new lover might have children too, so be warned – this can be a whole world of new and different trouble. Avoid trying to make one big, happy family until the relationship is strong enough to deal with it.

Answer questions about the new set-up truthfully, but chop them into bite-sized pieces for childish consumption. Don't be afraid to say that there are some things you're not prepared to talk about, and that everyone's entitled to a private life. Oh, and be prepared for the kids to throw this back in your face when you try to pry into theirs.

The step-parent...

...is one parent too many. Kids aged six and upwards know they have two parents, and even if one of them has died or is totally absent, they don't necessarily want or need a third, especially if it means having to put up with being 'bossed' around by yet another adult with yet another set of rules and boundaries. If you and your partner decide to move in together, get as much information as you can about living in a step-family. The dynamics multiply according to the number of family members, and what was once merely complicated becomes an unfathomable tangle of interpersonal relationships.

Step-families are hard to negotiate – very hard – and the biggest mistake most of us make is expecting to be able to do it without help, research or support. The problem areas are many, and because the subject of our kids is so highly charged, disagreements about them can turn on a pinhead from discussions into wars. Don't expect too much of yourselves or each other. If you're the parent, you will feel protective of your children, and that might sometimes appear over-protective to your partner, who is trying to build a separate relationship from the one you have with them. It's much too tricky to tackle here, but I will say that it's perfectly possible to make a happy, successful step-family if you're prepared to face the facts.

Note to parents

Your partners may never love your children the way you do, and expecting them to is unfair and unreasonable. However, you do have the right to ask them to respect your children and your relationship with them. Try not to interfere too much as they try to forge a relationship of their own with your kids. They're bound to get it wrong sometimes, and if they think you're going to jump down their throat for it, it will put them off trying again.

When they interfere in your parenting methods resist the temptation to explode at the audacity of it – they don't know how it feels to be challenged about our kids (unless they've got children of their own, in which case you might want to remind them how it feels). Stand back and give them time to resolve their own difficulties. Relationships take time to build, and if you constantly step in to fix things, they won't learn how to do it for themselves. Let your partner and your kids work things out in their own way. We'd all love an 'apple pie' family, but having unreasonable expectations will create disappointment and unnecessary hurt. Be gentle with everyone's delicate feelings, including yours, and don't take sides. Let everyone know they're loved and that they're all trying their best, and agree to make that good enough.

Note to step-parents

First of all, be kind to yourself: it takes courage to walk into an established family unit and try to forge a place for yourself within it. Be prepared for the fact that it takes longer than you'd think and that the kids may regard you with suspicion for what seems like an interminable length of time. It's not personal; it's just that you're taking something that has belonged to them – their parent's undivided attention. It will be frustrating and upsetting at times, but there'll be other occa-sions when they reward you with affection and small acts of kindness that make your heart swell with warmth as you sud-denly find yourself accepted.

Don't put yourself under pressure to become your step-children's new best friend, or use them to gain your partner's respect. If you try to force things in any particular direction, they are likely to resist and push against you. When they do push, try to deal with the issue yourself. Ask your partner's advice, but don't expect them to fight your battles for you. It's not fair to ask them to play piggy in the middle. Develop trust and mutual respect before attempting to discipline your step-kids, and always talk it through with your partner first. Be too heavy handed in your approach and you could blow all your hard work.

It's not a given that we will love each other's children, but we owe it to ourselves and them to try to face the issues as they arise instead of burying them because they aren't com-fortable or convenient. It's not easy taking second place in the life of the person you love, but when you love a single parent, second place is what's on offer because the children's needs always come first. If that feels unfair, it's only because they're not your kids. If they were, putting them first would come as naturally to you as it does to your partner.

One big, happy family?

It's when you and your new partner both have children that the fun really starts. As if trying to deal with the complexities of living together for the first time while building a relationship with a child who sees you as a competitor isn't bad enough, you then have to bring your own kids into the mix every other weekend and alternate weeks in the school holidays so that they can add their complex feelings too. As I keep saying, read up on it. Google 'step-parent' and you'll find lots of great sites offering support and advice. Try this one for starters: www. bbc.co.uk/parenting/family_matters/step_becoming.shtml.

Parental rivalry

Having no relationship at all with your ex is not a fair option if he or she is to have an ongoing relationship with your kids. It might suit the two of you to completely distance yourselves from each other, but it's the kids who end up paying the price. Most of us think that as long as we don't say anything bad about the other parent, then we're doing our duty in not ruining our kids' relationship with them, but that's not enough for 6–11s. If we really have absolutely no relationship with the other parent, the kids are free to play one side off against the other. But it's more likely that there is a relationship, albeit a hidden one, full of seething, unresolved resentment or hurt. It's these relationships that do the most damage.

Case: David and Annie

David told me how he discovered that his eight-year-old daughter Annie had been telling her mum all sorts of highly exaggerated and in some cases completely made-up stories about her weekends with him and his partner. To be fair, she'd also made up stories about life at Mum and Stepdad's house. It all came out one day after Annie told her dad – in front of his girlfriend – that her mum had said his girlfriend was 'ugly'. The girlfriend then insisted he confront his ex about her outrageous behaviour. It didn't occur to either of them at the time that Annie might have made it up, even though it's a pretty far-fetched notion that a forty-year-old woman would use a word like 'ugly' to describe another woman to an eight-year-old child.

David's relationship with his ex had been turbulent, and the split turned really nasty when she forced him to go through the courts for access to Annie, costing him thousands of pounds (his source of resentment). It had taken him years to get into an amicable access routine, albeit through gritted teeth, and he was terrified to do anything that might destabilise the situation as he believed Annie's mother to be a '…punishing control freak who wants me out of their lives altogether. Nothing I do right counts for any-thing.' He lived in fear of putting a step out of place and giving her an excuse to pull the plug on him seeing his daughter.

As far as his ex was concerned, she'd always been a single parent because he'd never been there for her and Annie (her source of resentment). 'He should be thankful I allow him to see her at all after the way he's behaved. He left me, remember, so now I suppose he's paying the price.'

Neither parent had let go of their resentment, and the anger they still felt towards each other was palpable, especially to Annie, who was the only person who still had a relationship with both of them. She knew that their smiles were fronts, and she saw straight through them. I'm sure that her lies started as a means of protecting herself from this dangerous adult dynamic. Children see things in black and white terms, so it would have made sense to Annie that loving her father in the face of her mother's anger might risk her disapproval. She might have felt disloyal and guilty towards her mother every time she allowed herself to have a good time at her dad's. The 'bad dad' stories she gave her mum will have been exactly what her mum wanted to hear, and she probably gave her daughter approval for them – for proving her own ideas right.

And in just the same way, when Annie told her dad stories about how her mum and stepdad always put their daughter, her half-sister, first she played right into her dad's worst beliefs about

TIPS FOR BEHAVING WELL WITH THE EX

♦ We don't have to pretend to be best mates – children would see through that anyway – but we do have to talk to each other about the kids, and they need to see us doing it.

♦ Arrange to have coffee once a month for a chat about the children, or speak to one another on the phone. If the absent parent is having problems, we should be trying to help because if it involves our kids, it's our problem too.

♦ Encourage questions and conversations about the other parent. It's important you give the children permission to carry on loving and feeling loved by your ex.

♦ Make sure they always have access to the other parent: put your ex's number on speed dial on the house phone.

♦ Check your motives before asking questions about life at their other parent's house. They are not our own personal snoops, and we might put them in a difficult position by asking them to spill the beans about our ex.

♦ Be interested in the stories they tell you about their life away from you, even if they're hard for you to hear. If they feel closed down by us, they might close down to us.

her mother, and he lapped them up, rewarding her with lots of sympathetic attention. She'd had them both eating out of her hands for years, not for any malevolent purpose, but to keep the status quo. Poor little Annie – she held the whole world in her hands, and the older she got, the more afraid she'd become of dropping it.

Neither Mum nor Dad was thinking of Annie. They were too busy investing in their old beliefs about one another, holding on to their 'proof' that the other was a worse parent. Annie didn't need them to say anything – she simply watched their facial expressions, the tension in their shoulders, and the edge to the calm tones they used with each other at the front door. There was no way to love both of them openly and keep them both happy. They unwittingly gave her no choice but to be sneaky about it. Once Annie's parents got together and talked it all through, they discovered she'd fed them years of lies and exaggerated truths about each other, which they'd happily accepted. Annie was acting in response to their behaviour. They had no one but themselves to blame.

I agree that two parents are better than one, but not necessarily that kids are better off living with them both at the same time. Couples either temper their beliefs for the sake of relationship harmony, or fight for the right to be right. Kids whose parents lead completely separate lives have to negotiate two sets of rules, expectations, boundaries, discipline methods and levels of consistency. While it might be hard on them at the time, I believe it's an advantage in the long run. Growing up with conflicting world views is great preparation for dealing with a world that has conflicting views. Having to learn to relate to both parents in their separate worlds is a bit like growing up bilingual: children learn to speak to each parent in their own language. They may be a little slower to learn to talk in the first instance, but when they do, they're fluent in two languages.

Children aged 12 upwards

When Harry Enfield's teen character 'Kevin' first hit our TV screens we all laughed and nodded our heads in agreement: this was what living with teenagers was like. One night you kiss them goodnight and send them off to bed in their cute animal-print pyjamas, and the next morning all you can get out of them is grunting, tutting, eye-rolling, sighing, foot-stamping and door-slamming defiance. It doesn't take only parents by surprise – the symptoms of adolescence creep up on the kids too, which is disorientating and frightening. Low moods, high moods, the desire for isolation, long silences, sudden rages, verbal attacks, diminishing concentration, increasing appetite, physical changes, extreme clumsiness (of foot *and* mouth) and oversleeping by hours and hours at a time... Imagine if we were suddenly to find ourselves suffering all these symptoms. Wouldn't we rush to the nearest doctor or psychiatrist for a diagnosis?

A 'symptom' is the body's way of letting us know that something's happening to it. If we think of our teenagers' behaviour as symptomatic of adolescence instead of the systematic destruction of domestic harmony, we'll have an easier time of it, and so will they.

L-plates

As my son grew up, I held on to the belief that parenting would get easier as he got older and more independent. It kept me going when things got tough, but it was just wishful thinking. Certainly, he became less needy of my minute-to-minute attention (he was happy to microwave his own burger and chips), but the issues he brought to the parenting table instead were big and complicated, adult-sized emotional conundrums that absorbed more of my time and energy than ever. I thought I knew what it was to feel powerless as a parent, but I was to discover whole new depths to it as he claimed his right to become the provisional driver of his own life.

Learners are all different. Some are reckless while others are cautious; some speed, others crawl; some love the feeling of freedom and others are terrified by it. Whatever learner our kids most resemble, we remain their teacher, overseeing, advising, troubleshooting, listening and encouraging them to do better, go further and be safe. At least that's what the job spec would say, but in the real world – between our jobs, other kids, relationships and a steadily returning life – being an understanding, readily available, patient and wise parent to a grouchy teen who 'doesn't care what you think', 'hates you anyway' and 'can't wait to leave home' isn't exactly a stroll in the park.

Is it in the job description?

So how are we supposed to cope when they're all mean and moody? How do we deal with their hormonal peaks and troughs? Are we really expected to stay calm and reasonable in the face of the chaos they bring to our life and heart? Fat chance, but then it's our job to give them something to push against while they practise flexing their muscles. Talking of jobs, it's not always easy to see what ours is, especially when kids get into their mid-teens. I felt like a chauffeur, maid, cook, cleaner, receptionist, bank, policewoman, judge, prosecutor, jailer, counsellor and teacher among other roles in relation to my teenaged son, which didn't leave much time to be his mum. For single parents who don't get to share the roles that our kids (cleverly) force us into adopting, it can be hard to 'keep on message', as the politicians say, and not allow ourselves to be distracted from the job in hand. It's not easy. Their lives and behaviour set so many emotional and practical fires that you can end up fire-fighting all day long, leaving little time for parenting.

The 'message' is that they are still our children, despite what they say, and as such need us to have faith in them. Our job is to provide them with our continued unconditional loving support, even when we don't like what they do, the way they look, speak or eat, or the people they hang out with. We need to keep our boundaries firm, but be flexible about where we set them. We need to back off a little and give them the space to make a mess of things, and resist the temptation to clean up after them. We need to allow them enough space to explore without giving them room to lose themselves.

Is it our turn yet?

The other thing that's happening around this time is that we start to feel a little freer to explore aspects of life that, as single parents, we didn't have time or energy for when the kids were younger – such as a career, social life and romance. Our desire to feel like real people with real lives once more can conflict with their need for us to stay put while they do a little exploring of their own.

I remember being very surprised when my son, aged 16, mentioned something in passing about the fact that he didn't like that I had been working so many evenings. 'But you're always either out with friends, in with friends, or locked in your room listening to music in the evenings. I never see you when I'm here,' I protested, feeling slightly irritated in response to what felt like guilt-tripping (which I was really prone to and he was really good at). He said, 'I know – I just like it when you're downstairs.' He didn't want to hang out with me, he just wanted to know that I was available if he needed me.

Despite all his protestations of maturity and independence, his needs weren't that different from when he was a little boy, and it was clear that my job was far from over. (He's now over 20 and I'm realising that no one was kidding when they said a child's not just for Christmas – or was that puppies?)

A return to tantrums

Among children aged 12–14 the craving for freedom, time away from us, acceptance, clothes, friends, popularity and romance is ferocious, and they want it at any cost. They will continue to need our approval on certain aspects of their life, but on most matters from this point forth our opinion will become very much a second or third consideration. If they're lucky, they'll be able to take our approval for granted because their burgeoning self-consciousness won't allow them to believe that anyone else thinks they're worth much unless they're trying very hard. Ask any 12-year-old what she most wants to be and she'll say '13'. That extra year promises to hold the key to a whole world of new possibilities. Kids aged 12–14 aren't that different from 15–16s in terms of their needs, desires and fears, but with much less freedom to explore any of their new curiosities, they are left confounded and frustrated. They haven't learnt any of the emotionally manipulative tricks of their older teen counterparts yet, so the only means they have of being heard is to shout, sulk and stamp their feet. It's like the terrible twos all over again, and requires the same handling. Read over the advice about tantrums on pages 109–11, as the techniques apply whether you're dealing with someone of four or 40. Obviously, the 'calm chair' isn't an option, but time out really comes into its own during the teen years. Avoid getting into arguments with kids this age because their logic and capacity for rational thought is underdeveloped, and trying to appeal to it when it's not really there will only frustrate you and make them feel stupid.

Young teenagers can believe that the whole world is against them, and they have some cause to feel that way. Society doesn't like young teenagers, and it doesn't cater for them either. They're viewed with suspicion and disgust. They talk too loudly in public and they swear. The boys are smelly and they're rough with each other. The girls shriek at glass-breaking pitch and wear clothes that would look more appropriate in a porn movie. They're oblivious to everyone else's needs, and behave as if the world belongs to them, and they're resented for it – I've seen it in the faces of people on tubes and buses. The thing is, it's true – the world really does belong to them: they're the next generation. They have everything in front of them and those who resent them for it are jealous.

I like this age group. It's full of vibrant, far-reaching and optimistic people who won't take 'no' for an answer. They're also vulnerable and unsure of themselves – unless, of course, they're surrounded by a pack of other self-conscious teenagers all trying to outperform one another, whereupon they become a faintly hysterical, overexcited mass getting heady with the power they're just realising they have over the world about them.

Square peg

If people were shapes, teenagers would be square. This is why they don't fit comfortably with us – their corners seem spiky and awkward, and they don't roll along with the rest of us. Later on, life rubs off the corners bit by bit, making them more rounded as time goes by. The only other shape a square can get comfortably close to is another square, and there's no place safer for teens than fitting squarely into a box with others just like them. Teenagers are desperate to fit in with one group or another for this precise reason. The fact that we might disapprove suits them perfectly, as it confirms what they and their friends already believe – that anyone over the age of 20 knows nothing of any relevance or interest to them.

There's no 'right way' to deal with this mindset; we just have to do our best to be as understanding as possible, and try not to be cruel in the face of what can sometimes only be described as ridiculous behaviour. My friend's 15-year-old son came back one weekend after staying with a pal and was sporting a dyed purple strip through his hair, like a skunk stripe over the top of his head. He looked at his mum and held his breath, waiting to see if she'd disapprove. He said, 'Well, what do you think of it?' She replied drily, 'Not much. You?' He replied challengingly that he thought it was great and he couldn't wait to show his mates. She looked furious, so after he left the room, I rolled up my sleeve and pointed out the tattoo on my right shoulder that she knew I'd had done when I was 15. She smiled – I had put his purple rebellion in context.

The science of being a teenager

Scientists have discovered that the human brain continues growing and developing well into our teens. They were able to deduce from scanning adolescent brains that the emotional part matures faster than the part that deals with logic and rationality. This explains why teenagers appear to understand the concepts of rules and responsibility, but don't actually think things through to a conclusion. They live for the moment, minute by minute. For example, a teenager is out with her friends and knows she has to be home by 10 p.m. or she'll be in big trouble. At 9.45, when she looks at her watch, she thinks she still has 15 minutes before she has to be home, so she carries on chatting. She has neglected to take into account the ten-minute walk home: she is unknowingly already late, but this information doesn't become clear until she looks at her watch again and realises for the first time that even though she is leaving at 10 o'clock, she won't be home until 10 past. 'Oh no, my mum's going to kill me,' she wails, and her friends take turns coming up with great excuses she could give for her lateness. By the time she's said her goodbyes and actually set off home, it's 10.10 and she's going to be 20 minutes late, so could well end up being grounded for the week. It seems unfair to her for two reasons: first, she remembered to look at her watch (big achievement), and second, she tried her best. She didn't flagrantly flout the rule – she just didn't think it through properly. It's as if the bridge between action (driven by emotion) and consequences (driven by logic) is missing, so the two can't be linked. Once that bridge develops, teenagers are able to understand the relationship between the two, but until then, they'll continue to behave in ways that appear baffling at best and stupid at worst.

Splitting headache

Parental separation during the teenage years is often more traumatic for the children than us, and can leave lasting scars on all concerned. Relationships don't usually end well, nor do they end for no reason. And while we might be able to protect younger children from the details, we can't hide the facts from a teenager, nor can we hide our feelings. They become unwitting and reluctant witnesses to our relationship demise and all the destructive consequences of it. The relationship between the parents has lasted many years, and the domestic environment is likely to be well established. For a teenager who has grown up with both parents, the concept of living apart from one of them might be unbearable. Young teenagers, just like their pre-pubescent selves, take everything personally, and it can be an uphill struggle staying on top of making sure they're not blaming themselves or holding themselves responsible in some way.

But that's not the main problem teenagers have to deal with after their parents split up. The real crisis comes when parents try to get their teenagers to side against their other parent, something most of us wouldn't even think of doing to our younger children, but don't seem able to help ourselves doing to our teenagers. A rubbish husband or wife could still be a wonderful mother or father, and as difficult as it might be to accept, our kids love their other parent, despite the ways in which that person might have hurt us or let us down. Making our children choose between us and them can be incredibly damaging. Testing their loyalty, gaining their sympathy, seeking their approval and encouraging them to take sides can tear a child apart. Leaning on children because you're lonely, hurt or depressed can be just as damaging because not only has one parent left, the other has abandoned their role as parent, expecting the teenager to pick up the pieces, or survive alone.

Case: Mark and Jenny

Jenny was nearly 13 when her parents split up. Her mum went to America and her dad Mark, she says, fell to pieces. She was 16 when she told me about it.

> I was really angry with Mum for going and for not taking me with her, and I wanted my dad to be angry too, but he was like a zombie. My brother said it was depression, and I felt sorry for him and everything...we were all upset, but it seemed like it was all about him. He did the washing, shopping and cooking, but when I tried to talk to him it was like, 'Hello? Is anybody home?' I got away with loads of stuff because he didn't notice the time, so I went to bed when I wanted and came in when I wanted. That was when I got in with a wrong crowd. They used to get me to steal sweets and make-up from shops. They said I was really good at it, so I stole bigger and bigger things to get more respect – until I got caught. The police took

*me home and my dad was really angry for once. He asked me
how I could do this to him after all he was going through, and
then the policeman said that I was probably going through
it too and sometimes kids do things for attention. I couldn't
stop crying. He was right. I thought my dad didn't care what
I did any more. He cried too and we both said we were sorry.
Things got a bit better after that.*

Jenny's dad, in his grief and depression, lost sight of his daughter
and how much she needed him after her mum left. By allowing
the rules and boundaries to slide, he made her feel as though he
was no longer interested in her safety. If he wasn't going to care
about her, then she wasn't going to bother caring about herself.

If you recognise yourself somewhere in this story, don't beat
yourself up – do something about it. Getting some counselling
will help support you through the split, show you how to deal
with your feelings better, and help you to take care of the kids
once more. If, like Jenny's dad, you don't do this, the situation
might come back to bite you.

They feel it – they're just not telling

Parents splitting up is not just stressful for those kids who
experience it during their teenage years: it's tough at other
ages too, but for different reasons. My son's father had all but
stepped out of his life completely by the time he was 12. In
retrospect, I should have fought harder to maintain their relationship and challenge his father's guilty denial of his son, but I
was busy focusing on my new relationship and, much as I hate
to admit it, it was convenient for me to have him out of the
picture. If I hadn't bought my son a mobile phone that year,
I'm not sure I would ever have found out how angry he was

over his father's lack of interest in him and how he blamed me for it. On his way home from school one day he sent me two consecutive texts that I've never forgotten.

Text 1: '2 boys av nickd my skool bag an pushd me in the river. Am soakd n muddy an they chuckd my trainers in 2. can u pick me up?'

Text 2: 'I'm really angry with dad. He shud av taught me 2 play football an stand up 4 myself then I wudnt get bullied all th time. If u didn't leave him, I wud be a stronger persn.'

I was really shaken. I had no idea he was having such a hard time at school, or that he felt so different from his peers with dads, but what really stopped me in my tracks was the way he'd connected the emotional dots. It was a far more advanced process than I thought him capable of. I still imagined his inner world to be made up of Chopper bikes, sweets, skateboards and Spiderman (well, perhaps not Spiderman). He'd never voiced an opinion on our status as a one-parent family before one way or another. As he'd never known it any other way, I assumed he wouldn't miss what he'd never had. I knew then that my assumption was naive and incorrect. I forwarded the texts to his dad and they began to build their relationship from scratch. It was uncomfortable for both of them for a long time, but they were committed and worked through it together. Eight years later their relationship is still slightly awkward, but they are two men who share a strong (albeit unspoken) connection, a mutual respect and a shy, tender love for each other.

Signs of teenage stress

Teenagers are pretty stressed most of the time as they take on the world (albeit a small one) without holding your hand. If you're worried that your teenager might be stressed as a result of the split – or anything else – here's a list of entirely normal teenage responses to life and the physiological changes taking place in their body and brain.

Sleeping

Teenagers need lots of this as their bodies do the growing while they're sleeping. They can regularly sleep up to 12 hours at a time, and need around ten for optimum performance. Sleep, and the lack of it, are problems for most families with teenagers. They won't go to bed early, but school means they have to get up long before they've had enough sleep. If your teenager is foul tempered, appears drugged in the mornings and can't eat breakfast, it's because, in terms of his night's sleep, 8 a.m. is still the wee hours.

Rebelling

Rebellion is all part of the separation process whereby teenagers claim the right to live their lives the way they want to and not how we would have them live it. They want to feel grown up, and expect to be treated as such, even if their behaviour does sometimes resemble that of a four-year-old (we're supposed to overlook that). Crossing our boundaries, pushing limits and taking uncalculated risks comes as standard, and as long as we insist that they take responsibility for the consequences of the choices they make, we need to give them the space to do it. Note: they're going to do it anyway, so the only decision we have to make is how smooth or rocky we're going to make it for them and us.

Challenging authority

They've taken our word for it for a long time. Now they're starting to think for themselves and are questioning everything, including our authority over them. Man, it's exhausting!

There's nothing you can say without the point being argued. The trick is not to argue (easy to say) unless you're in the mood to give them a good fight and have the wherewithal not to turn into a teenager while you do it (I just about got the hang of it by the time my son was 18). Avoid pulling rank too – 'Because I know better. Because you're a kid. Because I said so'. These are all ways of saying that you don't value your teenagers' opinion. If you're too busy to debate the point, say so, don't dismiss them.

Choosing isolation

Locking themselves in their bedroom for hours on end is also pretty normal teenage behaviour, although if they're not talking to their friends on the phone during that time, it might be worth asking if everything's OK. This solitary behaviour makes us worry, but we really don't need to because it doesn't last and it doesn't mean that they're suicidal, social outcasts, lost causes or anything else that comes to mind when we let our imagination run wild. They simply feel happier in their own company, where they can MSN with the only other people who understand them. It's not personal, even if it feels a bit insulting.

Being moody

I found my son's moodiness the most difficult thing to deal with during his teenage years. Although to be fair, I don't think his hormonal mood swings were anywhere near as bad or as frequent as my PMS. Again, don't take moods personally, even when they're directed at you. Of course you have to protect their siblings, but remember that if teenagers are in a bad mood, they're miserable and might need a tender word, even if giving them one is like reaching out to pet a snarling dog.

Feeling anxious

Some teenagers worry about everything, but this is more likely to be the case if they've grown up with a worrier – you! If you're an anxious personality yourself, you're unlikely to know how to help your anxious teenagers with their excessive worrying. Be sympathetic, but don't pretend to have the answers if you don't have them, and don't give advice that they know you don't take yourself. If you want to help them, you have to find out how by helping yourself first.

Being bored

If the mantra for primary school children is 'It's not fair', then the equivalent for 12s upwards is 'I'm bored'. Boredom becomes a universal word used to describe a whole range of emotions that they can't or won't identify. What it really means is that they can't find something to do that will sufficiently distract them from a world of things they don't want to think about – or they just don't have anything to do. More often than not, boredom is a desire to escape something we're feeling trapped by (money or freedom restrictions, lack of transport, rain, a bad mood and so forth).

Sex, drugs, alcohol and other fun

Not every parent will have to deal with their teenagers being involved in all three corners of the dreaded triad of parental fear, but most will have to deal with at least one. Times change, and what it was like when you were a kid doesn't really have much bearing on what's going on today. The drug culture in Britain is more wide-reaching than it's ever been; drug use is rife among young teens, and is no longer a way to spot delinquency. My best advice is get clued up so that when you talk to your teenagers you sound like you know what you're talking about. That goes for sex and alcohol too. Remember, do your freaking out away from them: they won't tell you anything if you're going to react badly.

Whose problem is it anyway?

If we recognise our own problematic behaviours starting to emerge in our kids (this is inescapable), we tend naturally towards one of two directions: we either try to 'stamp it out' in them before the problem grows as big as it has in us, or we ignore it and hope it'll go away. The former has all our good intentions behind it. We don't want our kids to suffer the same fate that we did, but leaning hard on an area that your teenagers know perfectly well that you struggle with will make them resent you for the hypocrite it makes you. Ignoring the problem is how your issues got so unmanageable in the first place, so ignoring theirs will not make their story end differently. Whatever your foible, whether it's temper tantrums, excessive worry, high achieving, low self-esteem, risk aversion/attraction, romantic delusions, money management issues, depression, pessimism, workaholism, emotional distance, sarcasm, phobias or any other difficult personality trait we might wish to save our kids from, it's too late – they already have the trait and they learnt it from us.

If we want to save them, we have to save ourselves. If we're lucky, they'll be watching how we do it, and the information will get stored away for the day they're ready to tackle it in themselves too. When they see us taking responsibility for our own behaviour, we earn the right to tell them to do the same.

If a self-help book doesn't give you the help and support you need, try treating yourself to some therapy sessions with someone who knows how to help you get a better handle on the behaviour so that you'll be able to deal with your teenagers' version of it – and your own.

Discipline from 12 upwards

As children grow through their teens, parents have less and less of a say over how they behave, who they see, where they go and what they do when they get there. There's no point fighting it; in fact, it's far better for everyone if we prepare to relinquish some of the control while maintaining our position as rule makers and keepers. There are no half measures when it comes to keeping teenagers in line. We have to be firm, fair and unfaltering.

Involving them in the rule-making process and the consequences of breaking those rules will give them a sense of responsibility that will make them much more likely to comply (or at least overstep them only by a short distance). It's called contracting, and can be done for each new event.

Contracting

Look at the following example of contracting (i.e. making a contract) with your teenager.

'You're welcome to meet your friends, but you have to be home by 9 p.m.' (Remember, there will be a bartering attempt, so choose a time you don't mind increasing.)

'But, Dad, no one else has to be in till half 10 or 11. Why do I have to be home so early?'

'What time do you think you ought to be allowed to stay out?'

'Half 10.' (So now the bartering is set: him 10.30, you 9 p.m.)

'OK, seeing as you did your homework on time this evening [rewarding good behaviour], I'm willing to extend the time to 9.30 – how's that?'

'How about 10? Pleeeease?' (10 p.m. is your bottom line anyway, but now you've got him on the back foot.)

'If – *if*, I say yes, *and* you're five minutes late home, what do you think the consequence should be?'

'You could ground me for a night.'

'And…?'

'No TV?'

'OK, if you're five minutes late, I will ground you for one night with no TV. Is it fair that if you're ten minutes late, you should be grounded for two nights without TV?'

'S'pose so.'

'Also, if you're more than 15 minutes late, you won't be allowed to stay out beyond 9 p.m. for two weeks. Do you agree?' (Now summarise.)

'So the deal is, you can stay out till 10 p.m., but for every five minutes that you're late, you accept that the consequences will be a night grounded without TV, and that if you're more than 15 minutes late, you understand that you will not be allowed out later than 9 p.m. for two weeks. Are you willing to accept the terms and conditions of the contract?'

Write them down if you think it might be more effective, or you can just shake on it, but make sure you have your teen's full agreement first.

It's also a really good idea to write a contract for house rules using a similar template, especially for those day-to-day areas you find yourself constantly nagging about.

Note 1: Protecting our kids from the consequences of their actions is false kindness. It's actually depriving them of an opportunity within the safe and loving environment of their home to experience what real life will expect of them. The outside world won't be so nice when it delivers the same message later on.

Note 2: The minute you don't carry through a consequence, you will undermine all your hard work. If you can't enforce a consequence for any reason at the time, explain why and then say when you will be enforcing it.

TIPS FOR MAKING A SOCIAL CONTRACT WITH TEENAGERS

♦ Let them negotiate: it's a good skill to learn.

♦ Be flexible, and be prepared to barter.

♦ Stick to your bottom line.

♦ Take each case on its own merit.

♦ Enforce the consequences exactly as the contract decrees.

♦ Be sympathetic if your teenagers have to bear consequences – it's not necessary for us to rub their noses in it.

♦ Let it go. There's no need to shout and rant if they get it wrong. Let them know calmly how you feel, and state what they agreed to accept as consequences. More often than not, they will take it on the chin. They might complain, but they're less likely to fight it if they agreed to it in the first place.

♦ Make sure you lavish them with praise and good consequences for getting it right. For example: 'I'm really proud of you for coming home on time. It must have been hard leaving your mates when you were having such a good time. I want you to know that I really appreciate being able to trust you like this. Thanks and well done.'

House contract guidelines

♦ Start by writing a list of the rules you want adhered to in your house. Leave a few lines under each one for your teenagers' additions/comments and amendments (at least show willing).

♦ Give them a chance to debate your rules, and possibly add one or two of their own. Having a say in what goes on in their home will give them a sense of responsibility and pride.

♦ Don't make more than ten rules; it'll be too much for them to remember, and we want them to succeed. Praising is so much more pleasurable that enforcing consequences.

♦ As a family, agree consequences for not obeying each house rule. (Make the consequences appropriate, reasonable and clear, for example: 'I agree that for every mug/glass found in my room on regular Saturday morning checks, I will hand over 20 pence of my pocket money.')

♦ Be prepared to behave by your own rules or pay the price when you don't.

♦ Include a reward system. For example: 'If a member of the family survives a whole week without a single consequence, he or she will get a free pass on a future 'crime'. This should be written on a piece of paper signed and dated by you for the person to produce at a time of their choosing – just like a 'Get out of jail free' card in Monopoly.

♦ Have a sense of humour, but let your kids know it's serious too.

What about school?

Schooldays certainly weren't the best of my life. In fact, they were some of the worst, and I know now that this is true for many others too. Social issues are of paramount interest to teenagers, and everything else falls in line behind them in terms of importance and relevance. Everything we do at school is in reaction to our social status, whether it's an effort to be more popular, get popular, hope nobody notices we're not popular, avoid being noticed, get noticed, make ourselves invisible, stand out, fade into the background, fit in, feel left out, included, excluded, liked, disliked... It's like being sent to our own personal version of hell every day for at least five years, although it tends to get better once we've established ourselves within smaller tribes around the age of 15.

Bullying

It's not easy to spot bullying, and those who suffer from it don't help by not speaking about it. I was bullied for a period of time in my mid-teens and I didn't tell my mum because I was ashamed. I didn't want her to know that I wasn't popular, that I wasn't liked, that I had no one to play with at break times. I thought she'd be disappointed in me, so I hid it from her and went home each day recounting happy excited stories that I made up on the train. She thought I was having a ball, so when I tried to pull out of the French trip she was baffled. I'd begged to go and had been desperately excited three months earlier when she'd said I could, but since then the lead bully had told me she was going to make my holiday a 24/7 hell for a whole week, and that no one was going to speak to me or sit next to me.

It took my mum and the head of year to crack me into

telling them the truth about why I was refusing to go. It was mortifying, and it got a lot worse before it got better: the headmistress and my form tutor got involved, the bully's mum was brought in, and finally the bully herself was forced to make a strangled apology in front of everyone. I felt so sorry for her. It was pretty awkward for a few days, but she never bullied me again.

Maybe if my mum hadn't been my only parent, maybe if she hadn't had to do so many jobs, maybe if she hadn't had four other children, she'd have spotted my distress earlier, but I doubt it. The important thing with teenagers is to keep your eyes open for odder behaviour than normal, and keep listening in case they drop a subtle hint that all is not well.

Teen talk

School is just one more thing we can't protect our kids from; they have to face it alone, but they don't have to feel on their own with it. Making space every day for the possibility of a conversation to take place between you and your teenagers – even if they rarely take you up on it – is one way of letting them know that you're there for them if they need you. Teenagers find it easier to talk if you're both engaged in a distracting activity, which is why they always seem to bother you when you're cooking or catching up on your emails. Do something ordinary with them each week that involves being active together, such as shopping, hanging out washing or baking cakes. That way they don't have to burn with self-consciousness under your curious gaze.

TIPS FOR TALKING TO TEENAGERS

♦ When they're talking try not to interrupt. The fact that they're sharing any part of their private selves is a privilege, and we need treat it like the delicate event it is.

♦ Be as honest as you know how to be when they ask you questions.

♦ Don't give advice; they tend to sound like orders from a parent. Make suggestions instead, and ask what they think they should do about their problem.

♦ Talk to them in an adult tone, but remember that they have no real experience to go on, so reduce the content to bite-sized pieces.

♦ Avoid dramatic responses as this will close them down too.

♦ Have faith in them. Believe that they will find their way through whatever the problem is, even if you're not sure how. If they suspect you don't believe in them, they'll think there's a reason not to believe in themselves.

♦ Be a fan, not a critic. The whole world's a critic, so you may be their only fan. If they feel you respect them, they'll demand respect from others.

Help!

1
2
3

s if the maze of emotional questions and complications isn't enough, being a single parent raises all sorts of practical problems. It has its own legal and financial implications, some of which can leave you feeling lost in a sea of jargon and official directives. The Internet is fantastic, but with so many different sites and so much information, it can be a bit overwhelming even to begin to know where to start looking.

To help you out, here is a list of cherry-picked sites for organisations, associations and companies that between them appear to have most of the answers. You might not need all of them, but I'm sure a few of them will be useful at some time or other.

Where to start

Single parents are still a disadvantaged social group, and as such we need to know our rights. The Internet was not what it is now when my son was little and I needed help, advice or information. I had to queue at the Citizens Advice Bureau (CAB) for it, usually with bored child in tow, so – I've always wanted to say this – think yourself lucky! I was of course grateful for the CAB, but back then it was almost all we had in the way of free resources. Nowadays anyone with a library card has access to the Internet and a world of information literally at their fingertips. (If you're unfamiliar with the ways of the web, check out your local adult education centre or college for basic IT courses to help you get up to speed – or you can do what I did and ask your eight-year-old to show you!)

There are more organisations, dedicated websites and grants available to single parents than ever before. However, as time is always a factor for single parents, be prepared with a list of exactly what you need to know so that you don't get sucked into the black hole of space and time that the Net can be.

Of course, support in cyberspace is no substitute for a real person who can help with your specific needs and concerns. This is where you'll benefit from a lone parent adviser at the Job Centre, a visit to the Citizens Advice Bureau (remember to take crayons!), or even half an hour's free legal advice from a solicitor who specialises in divorce, separation and family issues.

Don't be embarrassed to ask for help. Where was it written that we're supposed to know everything about everything and keep abreast of the changes? Admitting we don't have the answers is a big step nearer to finding them. Use this chapter as a starting point for finding out the basics, then follow up the websites or contact details for more specific, personally tailored advice.

Local knowledge is priceless. Ask teachers and other parents – someone is bound to know the answer to your query, or at least know someone else who does. This way you can find everything from the number of a good solicitor to details of a fantastic summer play scheme. Put out a few feelers and you'll be amazed how much useful information comes back. People like to help – it makes them feel useful.

Gingerbread (www.gingerbread.org.uk or 0800 018 5026) is a fantastic starting point. Not only does it have an incredibly well thought-out site, but it lists contact details of local groups that meet regularly. Look online for your nearest branch: there'll be one even if you live in a remote area. Another great site is www.mumsnet.com – invaluable when it comes to getting support from other parents.

A roof over your head

Shelter is one of the most basic human requirements. Few things are more frightening than feeling that your home may be under threat, especially when everything else seems to be crumbling around your ears. Certain relationship circumstances might make you feel like packing up the kids and leaving the family home, but unless you fear for your safety, or that of your children, don't. Possession is nine-tenths of the law, besides which, uprooting will be destabilising for both you and the kids. If possible, stay put – it will save you from enormous amounts of extra pressure. If, however, you do fear for your safety, or the situation is untenable because your partner won't leave, then go. Most courts accept that if the situation is impossible, or there's been violence of any sort, you may have to move out temporarily, and this shouldn't affect your claim. But before you go, take all your personal documents with you and make getting legal advice a priority.

If your home is not registered in your name, it might be possible to protect your interest in it by contacting the **Land Registry (www.landregistry.gov.uk or 020 7917 8888)**. Doing this ensures that your home can't be sold, or have charges placed on it against other debts, without your knowledge or consent.

Get expert advice

If there isn't a clear and financially workable solution that allows you and the children to stay in the 'matrimonial home' after a divorce or separation, it's vital that you consult a solicitor straight away. Your home is almost certainly your biggest financial (and emotional) asset, and your ex may therefore be very keen to put it on the market and share out the profits. If neither of you can afford to maintain two separate homes, this may be the only solution. However, the courts generally accept that the best outcome for children is to stay in the home with their main carer – you. If the house is jointly owned, your ex will be required to contribute significantly to the mortgage, regardless of your own contribution in the past. Make sure you understand your legal position as early as possible. If you have no other assets, your solicitor can help you to apply for legal aid, which may be repayable if and when the house is sold in the future.

Contact creditors

Any change in financial circumstances should be explained at the earliest opportunity to anyone with whom you have a financial agreement, including your landlord and mortgage, credit and loan companies. Some lenders can arrange a mortgage 'holiday', offering a couple of months' grace while you get on your feet, but if you keep them in the dark and they're unaware of the changes, they will pursue you as aggressively as they would anyone else – and that's pure stress. Do yourself a favour and protect your future as much as possible by phoning or writing to your creditors aware of your circumstances. It's awful to have to share such personal recent heartbreak with a landlord or moneylender who just wants his cash, but, in truth, the person on the other end of the line is human and therefore, in most cases, empathetic. All lenders say the same – keep them in the picture.

This is especially important when it comes to your home. If you have a tendency to bury your head in the sand over money matters, save it for the milkman, not your mortgage provider. Repossession is a relatively lengthy process, and most companies would much rather come to a mutually agreed arrangement for a limited period than to begin the eviction process. They won't just go away, so take the initiative and let them know that you're serious about your responsibilities, and stay in touch regularly with updates.

For more advice on how to deal with creditors and debt management go to **www.nationaldebtline.co.uk**.

Temporary housing

If the worst-case scenario happens and you find yourself and your kids standing on your best friend's doorstep holding a rapidly packed overnight bag and no money or other place to go, or you have your home repossessed, you will qualify for emergency housing, which might not be ideal, but it's a start. If you're homeless, or likely to become homeless, within 28 days, the housing department of your local council has an obligation to find you accommodation. Organisations such as **Shelter** (**www.Shelter.org.uk** or **0808 800 4444**) and the **Citizens Advice Bureau** (**www.citizensadvice.org.uk**) will advise you on how to apply for immediate support. There are also grants and housing association homes available to single parents in need of temporary accommodation, so don't assume the worst and resign yourself to sleeping on a friend's sofa for months on end.

Shelter offers masses of help and advice on all things housing-related, including special sections on divorce and housing rights. Another good site if you're at risk of becoming homeless is **www.Homelessuk.org**.

Are you entitled to housing benefit?

If you're on a low income and don't own your home, you may be entitled to Housing Benefit. Call the Housing Benefit department of your local council and make a claim as soon as you think you may be entitled because they will only make payment from the date you put in your claim. If you think you should have received benefit earlier, it might be possible in some cases to have it backdated, so explain your situation clearly as soon as possible. If you're renting from the council or a housing association, they should have a welfare rights officer who can help you. Whatever happens, don't stop paying your rent, as claims can take several months to process and you may not be entitled to the full amount. Check out benefit details online at www.direct.gov.uk because they change all the time.

Money

Aside from your children's happiness, your chief worry as a single parent is almost certainly going to be money: how to get it, how to make the most of it and how to handle debts. The never-ending stream of outgoings can have you lying wide-eyed and sweating through the early hours, just before little Johnny starts wailing for his breakfast. It's not surprising when new research suggests that raising kids costs an average of £23.50 per child per day. Money can feel like a mean taskmaster, but it doesn't have to be an enemy. The key to financial management is honest budgeting – you know, that list of incomings and outgoings that always makes you (well, me) wonder how the hell you've been surviving at all. I've found that the most important self-imposed rule when it comes to money management is 'Tell yourself the truth'. If you need help writing out a budget, visit www.moneyexpert.com, which will ensure you don't leave anything out.

Once you feel less stressed about your financial situation, involve the kids in the budget to give them a sense of what your household can afford. If they can see that there really isn't any money left, they won't pester you quite as much.

Use it as a guide so that they can understand you're not just being mean or making an excuse when you say 'We can't afford it'. But don't worry them or give them the kind of information that will leave them feeling insecure about their home and lifestyle.

Save yourself

In a recent newspaper article I read that if I saved the cost of my daily coffee-shop cappuccino and invested it wisely, I'd more than likely be a millionaire in 25 years' time. I'm sure it was just an attention-grabbing headline, and that I'd have to be an investment wizard to make that kind of fortune, but it made me think about savings. I was always told that the interest we pay on what we owe is greater than the interest we receive on what we save, so it is more prudent to pay off debts with any spare cash than to save it. Recently, though, I came across another suggestion. It said that when you get your money, pay yourself first, before bills and creditors. It only has to be a small amount tucked away into a savings account, but watching it grow has a strong positive effect on our sense of independence and faith in ourselves as money managers.

Money expert Martin Lewis has a website (**www.money savingexpert.com**) packed with great ideas about managing your money, together with regular updates on the best rates for loans and credit cards, and information about loopholes in the banking system that you might be able to use to your advantage. In addition, the site also researches special money-saving offers on your behalf.

Deal with debt

If your divorce or separation has left you drowning in debt, it's natural to panic, hide under the duvet or, worse still, take out a high-interest loan, but there are other options. First, prioritise your debts. Lower-interest debts, or ones that you can afford to postpone, aren't as important as covering basic services, such as gas and electricity, or mortgage payments. It's worth considering consolidating your debts (putting them all in the same place with one lender), but only if you're sure you can manage the repayments or remortgaging. Bankruptcy might be your best option, and isn't as scary or awful as it used to be, although it will have repercussions on your credit rating, and you won't be able to get any credit, hire purchase agreements, loans or a mortgage until your period of bankruptcy ends. Declaring bankruptcy is pretty drastic, so you should find out everything you can about it before even considering it an option. For some, even with all the disadvantages, it's worth it. The best thing you can do for yourself and your blood pressure is to consult a financial adviser, who will help put things in order. Most local councils have a free debt-management service, or you can contact **Clear Start (www.clearstart.org or 0800 138 5445)**, the national consumer debt helpline, which also offers free, impartial advice.

If you're more than £20,000 in debt, you should ask about an Individual Voluntary Arrangement (IVA). With this, a proportion of your debt will be written off, interest will be frozen and creditors will be kept at bay, so you're likely to have paid off what you still owe in around five years.

Plenty of independent financial advisers offer free consultations, and you can find one through websites such as **www.unbiased.co.uk (0800 085 3250)**.

Maximise your assets

Downsizing can be hard to accept emotionally. It's natural to want your kids to have the best, and it's not unusual to feel that you need to compensate for the trauma your break-up has put them through by saying yes to their many requests. But it's usually impossible to sustain the same lifestyle on less, or in some cases much less, income than was available when you lived as a couple. Debt is stress, so keep it to a minimum and maximise your assets instead. What this means is to have the same for less. You still have a home, but you buy something smaller or in a slightly less desirable area. You still run a car, but one with low fuel consumption and that's in a really cheap insurance bracket. Even the small stuff adds up. For example, in a standard UK household it's possible to save £37 a year in energy charges just by switching off electric appliances properly rather than leaving them on standby. I know!

However you downscale your lifestyle, try to keep a positive outlook on the whole thing, even if you don't feel it. Actually, what you're doing is positive – you are doing what's necessary to keep your family safe. You're doing your job. Keep your less-than-positive feeling about having to move or shop at a different supermarket away from the kids. Remember that for the most part they will respond as you do. Present the changes using bright, confident language and they'll follow your lead. Talk about 'new starts', get them excited about how they'd like to decorate their new rooms and find positive reasons for moving, such as a 'cosier' house that's 'nearer to Granny's' or closer to a park, and they'll find it easier to accept.

For great tips on saving energy and money visit **www. energysavingtrust.org.uk (0800 512 012)**.

Make friends with the bank

If you don't find your old bank sympathetic to your new circumstances, you're at liberty to take your account elsewhere at any time (unless you have an overdraft, in which case the

bank has a right to ask for it back in one go if you leave – petu-
lant, I say). Let them know that things have changed and that
you could do with some advice on how best to manage and
service your account. This will keep you in their good books,
and – let's face it – if we want to be in anyone's good books,
it's the bank manager's. One day you might need an overdraft
facility, or an extension on a current one, or a bank loan to
tide you over a tricky patch, so make an appointment with
your branch to discuss your situation and ask how the people
there can help. They're not the enemy – they're just part of
a big, mostly faceless corporation that doesn't second-guess
anything unless it's in their favour – so don't give them the
chance. Give them the facts and always respond to their letters or calls. If you find money management tricky, it might be
worth looking into moving all your money matters to the same
bank so that your adviser can see at a glance what's going on
with you financially.

Be a credit to yourself

The average cost of a divorce is £13,000. This includes legal
fees, maintenance and the cost of setting up two new homes,
and is the reason why few people embarking on life as a single or distant parent are financially comfortable afterwards.
Even if you've always been a single parent and haven't had
these particular costs to cover, there are others. As children get
older, they cost more, require more space and demand more
'stuff'. School trips, new shoes or trainers every two or three
months, winter coats, Christmas, holidays…and that's just the
kids' stuff. With constant financial pressures, it's not surprising
that credit cards look like the answer.

We live in a buy now pay later society, and the real concern is that while we know what we want to buy today, we

have no idea what the true cost will be tomorrow. Credit card contracts have small print stating that the terms and conditions can be changed as and when the company feels like it (OK, I'm paraphrasing, but this is more or less the case). I recently received notification from my own credit card company informing me that it was going to raise the rate of interest it was charging me by 2 per cent. When I phoned to ask why, I was told – because we can. I threatened to do a balance transfer to another credit card, and they retracted – temporarily. We wouldn't borrow money from someone who won't tell us how much we'd have to repay, would we? Why, then, do we accept such terms from credit companies? Because we're desperate, that's why.

I'm not saying that cards aren't useful. Used as short-term solutions to temporary problems, they can be life-savers – as long as you pay back the full amount in the shortest time possible. Unfortunately, according to the figures, this advice comes a little late, as most of us are already wrestling with high-interest plastic charges, but there's some great advice around for us too. At **www.moneysavingexpert.com** there's a list of the credit cards offering low-interest balance transfers for six months or more. Move your debt to one of these and you can pay the same monthly amount, but actually make a dent in it. Never pay just the minimum amount – it's often a paltry 3 per cent of the total debt, ensuring that you'll be paying interest for the longest possible time and playing directly into the card company's greedy hands.

The **Consumer Credit Counselling Service (www.cccs. co.uk or 0800 138 1111)** is a charity dedicated to providing confidential, free counselling on credit problems, covering all aspects of money management.

Can you benefit?

Plenty of single parents are eligible for extra benefits, so it's definitely in your interest to find out if you're one of them. Even if you own your home, you may still be able to claim benefits, depending on the hours you work and the money you have coming in. Contact the **Inland Revenue (www.hmrc.gov. uk or 0845 300 3900)** for information on single-parent benefits if you think you may be due Tax Credits. Some local councils have welfare officers who can advise about eligibility, but if yours doesn't, a local law centre should be able to offer benefits advice. And don't forget – there's always the CAB and your local **Community Legal Service website (www.clsdirect. org.uk or 0845 345 4345)**. In addition, the **British Gas Warm-a-Life scheme (0845 605 2535)** offers free energy-saving tips to people who live in private housing and are receiving any kind of income-related benefits.

Legal matters

Employing a solicitor isn't something most of us have to do every day, and some people will be lucky enough never to have that need. It's not something that we're prepared for, but in a situation where we're having to seek representation (probably because all negotiations with the ex have broken down), we need the strong arm of the courts to take over for us. The important thing to remember is that you're employing the solicitor. He or she works for you, so if they don't meet your needs, you can fire them and hire someone else.

If you're really unable to reach agreement with your ex amicably or otherwise, getting legal help can make the difference between a swift, simple order that will benefit the children, or an unsatisfactory situation dragging on for years.

Always get advice before you engage anybody, and pay close attention to what legal professionals tell you, even if it's not what you want to hear. Personal recommendations can save you having to mess around trying to find someone you feel you can trust, but remember, you don't have to like your solicitor as long as you think they'll be able to do the job. For a directory of solicitors specialising in family law visit www. divorceaid.co.uk.

The CAB can help with basic legal advice, but for anything complex it's essential to use a solicitor whenever possible. The CAB may arrange evening consultations with a solicitor for free, and many solicitors' practices will offer a short, free initial consultation in the hope that you will engage their services later on. You might find it's enough to answer your question, or give you a clue as to where to go next. Always ask about your eligibility for legal aid at the start of your interview, and be honest about your circumstances. It's possible that even if you don't qualify initially, circumstances might change and fees can be adjusted accordingly. If you can't get legal aid, solicitors' fees are usually from around £90 an hour. Be certain of exactly what you want your solicitor to do, and be aware that every letter, phone call and progress report may cost you money. Use their services only when you've exhausted every other avenue of negotiation: if you can come to an agreement with your ex regarding access or maintenance, do so. You can always pay to have it checked over by legal professionals before committing to anything. For copies of forms and leaflets relating to divorce visit the Court Service website (www.courtservice.gov.uk).

Whose side are you on?

Solicitors are completely uninterested in your emotional issues unless domestic abuse has been involved, or the divorce is being contested, but even so, they aren't counsellors. Their role is to get you the best deal. Don't waste time looking for a shoulder to cry on, or someone to validate your fury. Therapists are cheaper and better qualified to support you through residual feelings. The solicitor is there to work side by side with you to make sure your children's best interests are being met and not to punish your ex for being a lousy partner. Try not to let any personal anger or bitterness affect your financial or custody demands. The best outcome is that the children have a good relationship with both their parents, and a legal battle seldom increases the chances of that. For advice on child-related issues and the law visit **www.childrenslegalcentre.com**.

When is a court order necessary?

If you and your ex-partner can't agree on where the children should live, or on the amount of contact they should have with the non-resident parent, a court order may be unavoidable. As family law is so sensitive and emotions tend to run high, the court will usually appoint a **Children and Family Court Advisory and Support Service (CAFCASS)** officer to interview both parents and possibly the children to ask what they want to happen. (For information on the service and basic advice visit **www.cafcass.gov.uk or call 020 7510 7000**.) A court will make an order only if the judge believes it will be better for the children to have a clear decision made. If contact becomes an issue because your ex is breaking arrangements, acting unreliably in the children's company, or causing problems because of his of her unresolved feelings about your relationship, it may be advisable to use a child contact centre, which is a neutral meeting place. For details of your local centre, consult the **National Association of Child Contact Centres (www.nacc.org. uk or 0845 4500 280)**.

If you just can't agree

There may be one or two serious issues that you and your children's other parent are unable to agree on. If so, you can apply for a Specific Issue Order, which means the court will address only the issue in hand, which might be schooling, say, or a long-distance move. If you suspect the other parent is planning a unilateral decision, such as a change to your child's surname, or a move to a different school, you can apply for a Prohibited Steps Order, which means mutual agreement is essential before the proposition can go ahead. If you have reason to fear that the other parent might try to remove the children from the country, it's vital that you tell your solicitor straight away. It may be necessary for the court to make an order. It's also wise to keep the children's passports out of sight, and tell the school of your concerns.

The **Reunite organisation (www.reunite.org or 0116 2556 234)** can offer information and help to parents afraid that their children could be abducted. **Community Legal Service Direct (www.clsdirect.org.uk or 0845 345 4 345)** offers advice on all legal matters, and a directory of legal advisers.

Mediation

Going to court is the most stressful, expensive and unsatisfactory option for you, your ex-partner and for the children themselves. If there's any possibility of reaching a resolution before it's necessary to go to court, explore all the options, particularly mediation. Occasionally, the mediation service will be publicly funded, but more often you will have to pay – far less, however, than a court case will cost. It will usually consist of up to six 90-minute meetings in a controlled environment between you, your ex-partner and a mediation specialist, who will help you to explore the issues being disputed. Generally, the mediator will be a solicitor trained in conflict resolution or a trained counsellor, both of them able to channel and defuse painful emotions. If the situation is particularly tricky, it's sometimes possible to request two mediators at once. To get the most from mediation, it's important that you're both honest about your circumstances, and enter into it with at least a willingness to compromise wherever possible. Remember, the relationship between the two of you is over: you don't have to keep going over old ground. It's the new ground you need to cross together – for your children and your sanity. For lots of helpful information on mediation visit **Resolution**, the family law website (**www.resolution.org.uk or 01689 820272**).

Work matters

Fortunately, more and more firms understand the importance of accommodating single parents' needs, and the government has launched several schemes to help lone parents back to work without having to lose all their benefits. The key is to make sure you understand what's available, and never to assume that just because you're working a certain number of hours, or have a higher income than previously, you aren't entitled to help with childcare or bills. Feeling confident about who's looking after your kids when you're at work is essential, as is being able to leave early or take a day off when your child is ill. All these questions need answering, and luckily there's now plenty of advice and information available online to help you choose the right combination of career and childcare.

You may be concerned that taking a job with decent pay means that your ex will be expected to contribute less. This shouldn't be the case, but check with the **Child Support Agency** (**CSA**) at **www.csa.gov.uk or 08457 133 133** – still ongoing at the time of writing, but due to be abolished. As a single parent, however, work usually involves an uncomfortable or forced compromise. We need jobs that offer flexible or part-time hours, salaries that make paying for childcare worthwhile, and a working culture that makes room for the unpredictable. Options currently include job-sharing (where two employees share a single job), full-time work, part-time work, or working from home. Only 56 per cent of single parents are in employment, compared to a national average of 74.5 per cent, but the rate is going up, and if the current government has anything to do with it, all single parents will soon be expected to work once their youngest child is at secondary school, like it or not.

A fantastic source of information covering childcare, employment issues and advice on returning to work can be found on the BBC website (www.bbc.co.uk/parenting).

Back to work

If you haven't worked for a while, re-entering the job market can be daunting. It's immensely helpful to get as much advice as you can, so begin with your local Jobcentre Plus (www.jobcentreplus.co.uk), which has specialist lone-parent advisers. These specially trained staff can help you to work out the best hours and employers for your situation, and help you to apply for suitable jobs. If you're on benefits, you may be able to get help with travel or interview costs, so don't be afraid to discuss your requirements. The benefit of the government being so keen to get single parents back into the workforce is the pressure it puts on employers to adopt family-friendly policies, such as flexible hours, or time off during the school holidays.

Catch 22

The long-term catch for single parents has always been that if you work, you lose your benefits, so starting a job and paying for childcare and travel will end up costing you more than you make, and more than you received in benefits. However, Job Centre personal advisers can recommend you for a Job Grant – a one-off payment of £250 that you may be able to claim on starting work. You might also be eligible for a week's paid childcare to allow you time to sort out your own childcare arrangements. When you do get a job, you may qualify for Working Tax Credit, which lets you claim up to 80 per cent of your childcare costs back. If you work over 16 hours a week, you can't claim Income Support, but it's crucial to get advice on how much better off you may be from a personal adviser. For further information visit the Inland Revenue website (www. hmrc.gov.uk or 0845 300 3900).

Workplace rights

If you're in full-time or regular part-time employment and your child is under six (or 18 if disabled), you have the right to ask for flexible working hours, although your employer isn't obliged to comply, so I'm not sure how valuable that is. You have to be the primary carer for your children and have worked for your employer for at least 26 weeks. You're also entitled to paid and unpaid maternity leave, and unpaid parental leave if your child is under five. You're also permitted unpaid time off to deal with unexpected child-related emergencies. Most employers in large companies will be aware of the law, although you may need to remind them. In smaller companies, arrangements may be more ad hoc, but if you feel your employer is being unreasonable, unfair, or is possibly breaking the law, approach your union or the DTI for advice (www.dti.gov.uk).

Family-friendly workplaces

Some companies, such as Marks & Spencer, the Metropolitan Police and McDonalds, pride themselves on their family-friendly approach. Even the Inland Revenue offers flexitime, and attracts a lot of single parents as a result. With one in four British families headed by a single parent, it's increasingly important that businesses show their commitment to supporting parenting, so before applying for a job, try to research the company's record on benefits and support for parents.

Some large businesses have company crèches, or will allow you to take work home on one or two days a week. If getting to work and back just isn't feasible, it's worth considering an Internet business start-up at home, such as buying and selling on eBay. It's also possible to make a small amount of extra money filling in online surveys. These pay up to £12 an hour and there are usually two or three a month to complete. Try www.ciao.co.uk for details on how to sign up.

There's also the home parties option. Many major companies employ mothers to demonstrate their products at home in the evening when the kids are in bed. If you're interested, try Virgin Vie (www.virginvieathome.com), Ann Summers (www.annsummers.com) and the Body Shop (www.bodyshop.co.uk). Good sales people can easily make enough for a regular babysitter and a significant income working just one or two nights a week.

A great website that details family-friendly firms and practices, and has an awards scheme for the best, is www.workingfamilies.org.uk.

Childcare

In the hazy olden days when my single mum went to work, we were left with our grandparents during the holidays or when we were ill, but today's parents are often much older, and so are their own parents. These days Nana and Grandad are likely to be too elderly to take care of energetic youngsters, and the rest of our families have either moved away or are busy looking for someone to take care of their own kids so that they can go to work. Under modern circumstances, it's much more likely that you'll need reliable, affordable childcare, whether you're returning to work or forced to work longer hours because you no longer have a dual income. Even if you opt to work from home, it may be unrealistic to assume that you can get anything done when the kids are around, so a play scheme, part-time childminder or child timeshare (taking turns with another parent to look after each other's kids) could be the solution. If you work full-time, childcare is a priority, and you will need to do the research.

Childcare options

Feeling happy with your childcare is essential if you're a working parent. There are plenty of options in most areas, including after-school clubs, play schemes, registered childminders and nurseries. A qualified nanny is a very expensive option, and if it's just you and your child at home, he or she will benefit enormously from being around other children regularly. All childminders should be registered and be willing to answer all your questions, while nurseries should be able to produce an Ofsted report, which is a government report that measures a school's performance. All childminders should have completed a basic course in hygiene and first aid, while the care environment should be inspected every three years to make sure it's suitable.

If you're lucky enough to have relatives nearby who can care for your children, it's a good idea to assess whether they're able to cope with small children and if the environment is really suitable. However grateful you are to them, your child's safety has to come first.

Childminders can charge anything up to £6 an hour, and there are strict regulations as to how many children they can care for – a maximum of six, but only three under-fives. For older children an after-school club may be the best bet.

For wide-ranging information and advice on childcare visit the government website www.childcarelink.gov.uk or call 0800 096 0296. The Parentline website (www.parentlineplus. co.uk or 0808 800 2222) also offers comprehensive advice on all aspects of parenting, including childcare. In addition, there is excellent advice on what to look for in terms of childcare on the BBC website (www.bbc.co.uk/parenting) and from the National Childminding Association of England and Wales (www.ncma.org.uk or 0800 169 4486).

After-school and breakfast clubs

Many schools recognise the difficulty of parents having to work hours that don't tie in with the school day, so many of them now have clubs where children can be supervised. Most are held in school after hours, usually ending by 6 p.m., and children can draw, paint, join in games or do their homework. Although many clubs cater only for children aged 5–11, some will admit those aged up to 14, but any 14-year-old forced to spend more time at school than they have to, and hang out with little kids to boot, isn't likely to be happy about it.

Increasing numbers of schools also have a breakfast club for children whose parents need to get to work before school starts, and most do indeed include breakfast. Play schemes can also be a godsend in the school holidays. These offer kids organised activities and tend to run from 8 a.m. to 6 p.m., but that is a very long day for most children, so it's best suited to those aged about eight upwards.

All these options have a charge: up to £10 a day for after-school clubs and breakfast clubs, and £75 a week for play schemes – expensive, but in most cases more affordable than a childminder, although there's less flexibility. For example, if your child is ill, you will be expected to collect him immediately, no matter how inconvenient.

For further information about after-school clubs visit www.4children.org.uk or call 020 7512 2100.

Holidays

Single parents can find it a struggle to arrange holidays for themselves and their children, so thankfully various charities and organisations are available to advise on and even subsidise a holiday, usually in Britain. For example, Pearson's Holiday Fund (www.pearsonholidayfund.org or 020 8657 3053) is a charity focused on offering holidays to children who otherwise wouldn't get one. Similar help is available from the Children's Country Holiday Fund (www.childrensholidays.org.uk or 020 7928 6522) and travel companies such as Small Families (www.smallfamilies.co.uk or 01763 226567), which offer cheap deals and reductions for single parents.

Pre-school groups

Intended for children under school age, mainly between the ages of two and four, most pre-school groups (or playgroups, as they're often called) are run on a non-profit basis, often by parent management committees. Sessions usually last 2–4 hours and cost about £3.50 a time, though if you're on benefits, your child might be entitled to a free place. Groups are inspected every year to make sure they're up to standard. At least half the staff should be trained, and many offer an 'early years' curriculum. As the sessions are short, it can be difficult for parents to base part-time work around pre-school, particularly as most close during the holidays. These groups are best used as a means of social interaction for the children and to give you a short break. The **Pre-school Learning Alliance (www.pre-school.org.uk or 020 7833 0991)** offers advice on all aspects of pre-school.

Subsidised childcare

From four years old up to school age children are entitled to free part-time childcare at nursery, playgroup or pre-school for a certain number of hours per year. If you're on a low income, your child may have a place at a community nursery subsidised by your local authority, although demand for places is often very high, so there may be a waiting list. You'll also need to live within the nursery's catchment area, but as a single parent on a low income, you might get priority treatment. To get a subsidised place at a local authority nursery, you will need to be referred by your health visitor or social worker. If your child is disabled or has special needs, you will be offered free or subsidised services automatically.

Further help and advice is available from the **Daycare Trust (www.daycaretrust.org.uk or 020 7840 3350)**, a national charity that promotes free childcare.

Tax Credits and the New Deal

Child Tax Credit (CTC) and Working Tax Credit (WTC) are benefits for families on mid- to low income. CTC is paid whether or not you're working and is in addition to Child Benefit, while

WTC can help with childcare costs if you're in low-paid work. CTC can be paid on incomes up to £58,000, while WTC is paid if you're working over 16 hours a week. As a single parent, you'll be entitled to a higher rate as long as you're on a low income, and you may be able to claim back a significant proportion of childcare costs (see Workplace rights, page 181.)

While you're looking for work, don't forget the **New Deal for Lone Parents (www.inlandrevenue.gov.uk or 0845 300 3900, and www.newdeal.gov.uk or 0800 868 868),** a government initiative that offers support with training if you're receiving income support and your child is under 16. During a period of job-seeking or training, you could get up to £135 a week for one child, or £200 a week for two, to cover basic childcare costs and transport.

Help is out there for a reason, so don't feel embarrassed or awkward about using it. No one is expected to be fully genned about everything, which is why so many of the organisations mentioned here tend to specialise. When there's so much help and support available, it's madness to struggle on alone without using it – and yes, that is my professional psychotherapist opinion!

The last word

When I was first approached to write a handbook for single parents, I was flattered, excited and triumphant. My son was about to turn 20, I was about to turn 40 and we had both 'survived' our experience of single parentdom. It had been a long and often hard uphill struggle, but somehow, with very little guidance or support, we'd come through it relatively un-scathed and I was feeling comfortably smug. The process of writing this book certainly put a stop to that. While I was busy advising *you* not to feel guilty, I had to attach a note to my computer that said 'You did your best and he's great!' because every time I wrote down a suggestion or made an observation, I'd remember how wrong I had got it with him when he was younger, especially in his early years. It's for this reason I want to say that no matter what you do, how wrong you might have got it at times or what kind of mistakes you will make in the future, not only will children survive the worst of your parent-ing, but they will choose to forget much of it. What will stay with them is the fun you had, the giggles you shared, the hugs and kisses, the times you were patient and understanding, your pride in their everyday achievements, and the feeling that you will always be there for them whatever the circumstances. When they look back over their experience of being your child, these are the memories that will take precedence.

I know this because during the writing of this book I interviewed dozens of older teenagers who grew up in one-parent families, and while they remembered the hard times and difficult moments, what they wanted to tell me about was how proud they were of their single-handed parent and how loved they had felt by them. They were aware of the sacrifices their mums or dads had had to make, and they were grateful. They were able to put their parents' occasional 'bad' behaviour in context with their situation and accept that they had sometimes got it wrong without judging them for it. Our kids judge us only if they feel we're purposely withholding something from them that they need – such as our love, acceptance, forgiveness or an apology. What they want is to have a good relationship with us, and they won't let old resentments get in the way as long as we don't either.

In my capacity as a media pundit and 'expert', I'd got used to discussing parenting issues using broad brushstrokes rather than the magnifying glass that writing this book required. Having to talk in soundbites for TV programmes or write in punchy paragraphs for newspapers and magazines meant that I never had to look at anything in such a way that would mean really 'lifting the lid'. Writing this book did more than that – it blew it right off! I had no idea until I wrote this handbook just how much the person I've become, the decisions I've made and the way I feel about myself and my place in the world were steeped in my experience of growing up in a single-parent family and of being a single parent myself. I do now, and it's given me a new sense of pride and pleasure in our little family. It was by no means plain sailing, but we made it, my boy and I, and so will you.

From the bottom of my heart, I urge you to have faith in yourself *and* in your kids. Forgive yourself for the mistakes that you will surely make, and give yourself another go at getting it right next time. Banish guilt at every juncture, but listen to your conscience: it's wise, and if it comes knocking, it's probably got something important to say. Get a life, preferably one you enjoy, and remember that as long as your kids feel loved and feel sure there's nothing they can do to change that fact, they and you can't go far wrong.

Good luck and all the best.

Index

Acknowledgements

To my brother and sisters – if I said 'Thanks', you'd say 'What for?' and how would I even begin to answer that? Anyway, you so know already.

Thanks to Ed for never letting go of our hands. We're still holding yours too.

Flic, thanks for your unbending faith in me (I never doubt myself around you) and for getting your hands dirty to help dig me out of the holes I keep digging myself into…

Simon, thanks for sharing your wife, family, holidays and home with me.

Matt, you once thanked me for bringing up our son so well despite the odds against – I never told you how much that meant to me. All's well that ends well.

To Vin, you found yourself a single parent overnight and under the worst possible circumstances. Thank you for taking over and for trying so hard.

To all the single parents who contributed to this book – and their beautiful, enriched, soulful, sensitive, tough, bright, adventurous, affectionate, daring children – thanks for spilling all the beans: the good, bad and ugly! Especially Lisa, Georgie and Harriet, Wolfie, Mimi, John and Megan, Kiki and Bibi, AJ and Emily, Emma and James, Janey and Pete, Toni and Derek.

Special thanks to Sasha Baveystock for letting me help with Teddy's ketchup issue, for giving me the job on *Little Angels* anyway, and for putting my name forward for this book.

And to the rest of the *Little Angels* team, particularly Clare Beavis, Blue Ryan, Juliet Singer, Sue Davidson, Tanya Byron and Stuart Murphy. I feel proud and honoured to have been a part of something so important. Thanks to you and the dozens of other essential players for making it such an amazing experience and for paving the way for this book.

Thanks to Ann Kearney for never losing her nerve with me, and to Janet Tolan for watching my back. To Toni Lee for trusting me with myself, and Lisa ML for making me laugh no matter how hard I was crying. Thanks to Jane Wood for always being on my side, and to Emma Shackleton for letting me grow her idea and present it as my own!